pocket
essentials

La primera Imprenta en América se estableció en la Ciudad de México, el año de 1539.

typography
pocket
essentials

ILEX

TYPOGRAPHY POCKET ESSENTIALS
First published in the United Kingdom in 2014 by
I L E X
210 High Street
Lewes
East Sussex BN7 2NS
www.ilex-press.com

Distributed worldwide (except North America)
by Thames & Hudson Ltd., 101A High Holborn,
London WC1V 7QX, United Kingdom

Publisher: Alastair Campbell
Creative Director: James Hollywell
Managing Editor: Nick Jones
Art Director: Julie Weir
Designer/Editor: Graham Davis

British Library Cataloguing-in-Publication Data
A catalogue record for this book is available from
the British Library

ISBN: 978-1-78157-115-6

10 9 8 7 6 5 4 3 2 1

Printed in China

Colour Origination by Ivy Press Reprographics.

Introduction

Before type

History of type

Serif masters

Display type

The new century

Sans-serif

Back to the future

Digital type

Anatomy of type

Font identifier

Reference

Introduction

The evolution from the written word into the printed word has resulted in the discipline that we call typography. The term covers both the design of typefaces and their use in visual communication. Typography has seen many technical advances, the most recent of which being the digital revolution. It is therefore a paradox that in an industry that depends upon the very latest technology, many of the typefaces that we use today were created hundreds of years ago.

Typography could not exist without the invention of the "printing press." But it is movable types and the process of their manufacture that is responsible for the advancement of printing. These cast metal letters that could be used again and again were the basis of Johannes Gutenberg's eventual breakthrough—the "soldiers of lead that have conquered the world," as they have been called.

Typographers and printers have always been occupied by the merits of this or that typeface, but now the writer of a "thank you" letter, who once took up a fountain pen, can sit at a keyboard and scroll through a collection of fonts, choosing one at random with no knowledge of its origins.

Among the thousands of digital fonts now available are the classic typefaces from over 500 years of printing. These were innovations in their time, setting standards, and each has a story to tell.

The heart of the story lies with the punchcutter, who with simple, unremarkable tools but with the skill of his hands and the conviction of his eye, by the tightening of a curve or the thinning of a serif, was able to transform a commonplace letterform into a character of unique personality.

At first, typefaces were cast from a mold that was fitted with a matrix, so that when the molten metal was poured into the mold, the reversed, indented letterform of the matrix dictated the type's shape. A matrix is a die of a single type, and a punch is required to make it.

The punchcutter starts with a small bar of steel, out of which he will cut a punch for each character of a font—capitals, lower case, figures, and punctuation. If a character includes an enclosed space, like "O," "B," or "a," in one technique of punchcutting, a counterpunch may be required. This is cut to the shape of the enclosed space and driven into the letter punch. Then, passing the punch over a lighted candle to coat it with soot, he presses it onto paper, to ensure uniformity with the style of the other characters. When complete, the set of punches is hardened. Any number of matrices could be made by the process of a "strike," when a punch was driven into a small bar of copper. These were then trimmed, ready to fit into the mold.

Gutenberg's most signifigant invention was an adjustable mold, which would fit to the character widths of different type sizes. With the matrix fitted, a small amount of molten metal was poured into the mold, and within seconds a piece of type could be removed. Although modified and refined this process lasted for over 400 years, until the late 19th century when Linn Boyd Benton invented the punchcutting machine.

During the 20th century the skills of type design moved from the punchcutter-designer to the draftsman-designer, using digital outlines, described in the form of Bézier curves. Using this method, many new and innovative typefaces have been created, ushering in the start of a new era in type design and typography.

Much of the terminology we use today comes from the days of letterpress printing—like "body," the piece of metal out of which the character was created, or "leading," which derives from the strips of lead used to add interlinear spacing—and digital technology has added to this lexicon with terms like "font metrics" and "style sheet."

In the following chapters we look at the history of type design and the great names associated with it, as well as the anatomy of individual characters. We explore what makes type look good on the page or screen; and finally there is a font identifier that will help you select the right typeface for your next project.

BEFORE TYPE

THE EVOLUTION OF LETTERFORMS

THE ALPHABET we use today in America and Western Europe is derived from the Roman inscriptional letterforms of the first century AD. One of the finest examples of these letterforms is cut into the plinth at the base of Trajan's Column in the Forum in Rome, erected around AD 114 as a monument to the exploits of emperor Marcus Traianus.

The evolution of letterforms

The Romans adapted their alphabet from the Greek system of writing, and the Greeks had modified the Phoenician system by adding letters to represent the vowels. The Trajan's Column inscription contains most of the letters of the alphabet we use, but the early Roman alphabet did not contain the letters "J," "U," or "W." The letter J was not introduced until the 17th century, because it was not previously differentiated from the letter "I."

These chisel-cut letters are known as quadrata or, more commonly, square capitals. The techni-cal term for these letterforms is majuscules. These capitals were used to express authority, as they do today, and their form contains the structural proportions that still inform the basic proportions of our current lettering and typefaces. Look at the full forms of "O" and "D," and the narrower forms of "E" and "S." Such forms represent classical proportions, geometric relationships of form established by ancient Greek and Roman cultures, which have become ingrained in our letterforms and have been returned to time and again for inspiration through

Square capitals are the origin of our present-day alphabet. Note how the serifs, which are not crucial to the identity of the letterform, seem to derive from the nature of the broad pen or brush.

history. They are examples of the origins of the European cultural aesthetic.

These letters would have been carefully drawn out and then cut into the stone, and therefore represent permanence and formality. This is in contrast to the handwritten form, which can be formal but also informal, created in a more immediate way on wax or papyrus, which is, of course, less permanent.

An important feature of Roman letterforms is the serifs, the small cross-lines that complete the end of a stroke. Their existence has been the subject of academic study, as their presence does not have a bearing on the letters' meaning since the letters function perfectly well without them. The Roman Catholic priest, teacher, and calligrapher, Father Edward Catich's explanation has general acceptance, which is that serifs are formed as a result of the scribe drawing out the letters with a brush as the panel was planned, before the mason finally cut them into the stone. This would explain the bracket-like shapes formed in the example below.

While square capitals were for monumental inscriptions, there was also an informal handwritten version of the capitals for ordinary occasions. This form is known as rustic. These more condensed forms appeared during the second to fourth centuries AD. Although there are examples of carved rustics, it was a form used largely for the recording of more ephemeral information—everyday documents such as contracts, bills of sale, legal, and domestic letters. Literary manuscripts were also written in rustics, for example Virgil's Aeneid.

UNCIAL EVOLVES

During the fourth century, rustic capitals were modified to a more rounded form, adapted to the convenience of writing with a pen. A form known as the uncial (from the Latin for "inch") gained success over the rustic because it was easier to read. The handwritten form using a broad pen created a broad, vertical stroke that contrasted with the thin, horizontal stroke as the pen was moved across, up and down, and up and round.

Right: Trajan's Column is a second-century Memorial to the Roman Emperor Traianus. Pen-written square capitals were used for a variety of documents, both formal and informal.

MNOPQRSTVX

MNOPQRSTVX

The evolution of letterforms

Left: A French manuscript illustration from 1340 shows a scribe seated at his writing desk with his tools. The exemplar from which he is making a copy is open on the stand before him.

Above: The Luttrell Psalter from 1320 demonstrates the strong, vertical strokes of a broad pen and was completed separately to the illumination, despite the integrated appearance.

Further changes came about over time as the hand and pen dictated the form more distinctly. A preference for curves brought about the more economic half-uncial, creating the minuscule form. From this development, one can see the first signs of what is, in typographic terms, the lowercase letterform.

THE HALF-UNCIAL

The half-uncial flourished throughout Europe because of its use in mostly religious works. It developed regional or national styles, each with distinct characteristics that made it possible to identify its place of origin: the Merovingian style referred to France, the Beneventian to Italy, the Visigothic to Spain, and the Insular to Ireland and England. One of the greatest achievements of the art of the scribes and illuminators of the period is the Book of Kells, a beautiful product of an Irish monastery, which contains a Latin version of the Gospels and dates from approximately 800 AD.

CHARLEMAGNE

The Holy Roman Emperor Charlemagne (742–814) had united most of Western Europe by 804. He intended to consolidate the Christian faith by reforms that included the establishment of a system of education, and the patronage of the arts and literature. He was concerned at the diversity of written hands throughout his Empire, and as

Above: Many years of use and the increasing importance of writing caused modification of the square capitals, so that by the fourth century a more cursive form evolved. This later became known as the uncial. Note the circular form of the "e," heralding the development of the lowercase letterform.

part of his reforms he commissioned Alcuin of York to set up a new scriptorium at the Royal court in Aachen, now in Germany, where he was to create a script to become a new standard for manuscript writing throughout the Empire. It was based on the Insular half-uncial and the Merovingian hand. The new script has become known as the Carolingian script. It was a ninth-century attempt to improve communication by the introduction of standardization.

THE MONASTERIAL AGE

From the fall of Rome in the fifth century through to the 12th century, monasteries and other establishments related to the church had a monopoly on book production, and were therefore able to control the content and circulation of manuscripts. For many centuries, manuscripts were the only written medium for recording and conveying ideas. The place where the manuscripts were copied was called a scriptorium and most scriptoria were attached to a church or a monastery. The work of the scribe was to copy religious manuscripts, Bibles, and books of prayer. Most original exemplar manuscripts were owned by

Left: During the sixth century, the half-uncial was established as a forerunner of the present lower case. Note the triangular form of the "a" has modified into a continuous circular form. The tail of the "G" has also lengthened considerably.

The evolution of letterforms

the libraries of the church, or by nobles, and were loaned out to the scriptoria for copying. People employed as stationers were responsible for recording the loans of the exemplar manuscripts and checking that they had been copied correctly.

SECULAR SCRIPTORIA

From the end of the 12th century, the church monopoly was challenged as universities established their own scriptoria. Although the monasteries continued to produce manuscripts for their own devotional needs, the establishment of the new universities, and the development of learning among the laity, created a new kind of reader.

After the monasterial age, the secular age brought only small technical changes. The major innovation was the introduction of paper. Traditionally, books and other manuscripts were written on parchment, which was expensive and depended on an adequate supply of animal skins. The universities' growing demand for books made the expanding manufacture of paper an alternative to be encouraged, especially as the students required a less elaborate product.

REGIONAL SCRIPTS

During the centuries following the introduction of the Carolingian script, the influence of Charlemagne's revisions began to fade and regional writing styles slowly began to reappear. In northern Europe there gradually emerged the group of heavy, solid, manuscript hands called Gothic

Above: A Chinese drawing depicting two papermakers preparing paper. The wet sheets of pulp were smoothed onto screens to dry out.

or blackletter. Textura was one of this group, and by the early 15th century, with minor variants, it was a standard script in German-speaking regions for formal book work. It was on the Textura letterform that Johannes Gutenberg based his first type designs. "Gothic" was the disparaging term used by the Renaissance humanists of Italy, who had, through the church bureaucracy, reintroduced a form of Carolingian script that was considered to best reflect the values of humanist philosophy.

THE BIRTH OF PRINTING

The production of books written and illustrated by hand was a highly organized but slow and labor-intensive process. By the 15th century, the demand for books was increasing. Printing from a raised surface had been known for many years, but only from woodcut blocks, not individual letters. At markets and fairs it was possible to buy block books—booklets printed from woodcuts, with pictures of religious events illustrating a short, handcut text. Making prints from a raised and inked surface (letterpress printing) is the oldest method of printing, and it maintained supremacy over other methods of printing well into the 20th century.

Many technological advances depend on the coming together of a number of new developments. In the case of printing, it was paper that played the key role. Compared to parchment, paper offered a suitably manageable and more economical material for printing.

Papermaking was a craft that originated in China, and is believed to have been the discovery of Cai Lun in AD 104. The first papermill in Europe was established in Catalonia (now in Spain) in 1238, followed by mills in Fabriano in Italy in 1276, and in Nuremberg in Germany in 1389. Papermaking required specific conditions to operate effectively. The mills needed to be near water for power and for processing; and they also needed to be near a sustainable supply of rags, which were then the basic ingredient of paper, so the mills had to be close to large population centers.

Above: An eighth-century text from Alcuin of York's Acts of Council of Ephesus. Note the use of initial letters in this uncial-formed alphabet.

Below: An illuminated initial letter from the 14th century. Within the letter, a monk is shown writing a manuscript.

HISTORY OF TYPE

THE RENAISSANCE

2

THE MIDDLE AGES had seen the collapse of the Roman Empire and the consolidation of Christianity throughout Europe. By the 15th century, feudalism, previously the dominant social and economic structure, was beginning to give way to a monetary economy.

The main thrust of the Renaissance was the rediscovery and admiration of the ancient pre-Christian cultures of Greece and Rome, and a new belief in the value of those artifacts and manuscripts that had survived into the 14th and 15th centuries. The ancient civilizations offered knowledge of every aspect of human endeavor: art, literature, architecture, engineering, philosophy, medicine, science, and government. The integration of Greek and Roman knowledge and wisdom with Christian morality brought about the concept of humanism.

The humanist ideals were individualism, originality, and a general proficiency that was the basis of Renaissance education. This was expressed in the importance attached to the visual arts; these were patronized by the church, rich merchants, and dignitaries, so that they developed from workshop-based artisan activity to the heights of creative skill and imagination.

At the same time, the developing international trade created an increasing number of successful merchants, whose power and economic importance brought about the institution of banking. Although forbidden by the church, the desire by the wealthy and powerful to make use of credit and to possess and consume goods, was supported by an increasing reliance on loans with interest or concessions.

It was in the climate created by the two driving forces of commerce and passion for knowledge that the invention of printing from movable type was to grow so quickly. Even though printing could provide classical and religious texts for an increasing audience at a more acceptable cost compared with handwritten manuscripts, printers and publishers needed considerable financial support as printing a book was an expensive undertaking.

Opposite: In his notebooks Leonardo da Vinci represents the Renaissance man as being someone with a vigorous interest in all things. Beginning in 1508, he kept notebooks, writing notes and treatises in them, and making drawings on many subjects, from the mechanics of war to anatomy. As he was left-handed, he wrote using "mirror writing" from right to left.

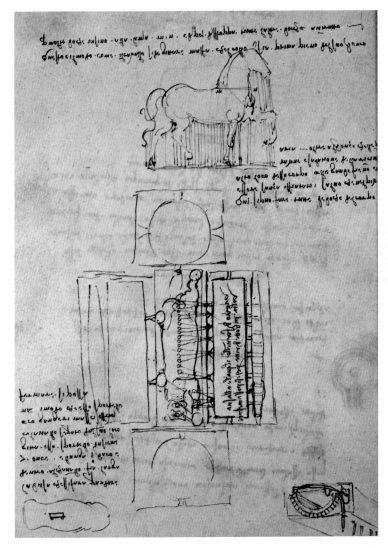

THERE IS CONTROVERSY surrounding the origin of the invention of printing from movable types in Europe. However, it is generally accepted that between 1440 and 1450 Johannes Gutenberg produced the first-known book to be printed in this way.

Johannes Gutenberg

Little is known about Gutenberg. He was born in the German town of Mainz, capital of the Rhineland Palatinate, in about 1394; he lived for some time in Strasbourg, and died in Mainz in 1468. What we do know about him is derived largely from the court records in Mainz, at the time a city of 6,000 inhabitants.

It is likely that Gutenberg employed a number of people to help him with the development of his printing invention. This possibly led to the financial problems that he experienced during the years of his research and development. The court records refer to a legal dispute over a loan of 800 guilders. The loan for "work on the books," was made by Johannes Fust, a lawyer. A further loan of 800 guilders was made, which also named Fust as a partner. It appears that in 1455, Fust decided to take over Gutenberg's invention rather than accept the return of his investment, which would suggest that Gutenberg was enjoying success with his innovation. Fust continued printing in partnership with Peter Schoeffer, originally Gutenberg's foreman. Schoeffer had a good knowledge of the printing process, and later married Fust's daughter. After the loss of his types and presses, little more is known of Gutenberg,

The 42-line Bible, Gutenberg's masterpiece, was completed c.1450. The design consisted of two 42-line columns per page. Also known as the Mazarin Bible, and printed as two volumes, it contains some 1,200 pages. About 180 copies were produced, of which 48 are known to have survived to the present day.

Vorrede in das Bairisch lantrechtbůch.

Ir Ludwig von gottes genaden Mar/
graue tzů brandenburg. Wir Stephan.
Wir Ludwig. Wir Wilhalme von gottes
genadé Pfaltzgrafe bey rein vñ Hertz/
og in bayren ꝛc. Habé angesehen den ge/
preste den wir gehabt haben in vnserem
lande tzů bairen an dem rechten. Ánnd
dauon sey wir zů rat wordé mit vnserm hertzé vñ vätterlein
taiser Ludwigé vó rom. Áñ setzen vñ bestätige alles das
hernach geschriben steet nach seiné gebot vñ haissen vnse
rem land zů bairn zů füderug vñ zů funderé genaden. Das
ist geschehé do man zaltvó cristi gepurt dreusehenhúdert
vnd in dem sechfund viertzigsten jar des nächsten sam̃f/
tags nach dem obersten ꝛc.

Wie man dz recht behalté sol.

Da von gepieten wir bey vnseren hulden allen vn/
seren Richtern vnd Ampleuiten in vnserem lande
tzů bayren überal jn stetten vnd merckten vnnd auff dem
land Das sy die selben recht also behalten bey iren ayden
die sy vns od vnsern victzumb darumb schweren müssen
Ánd das sy darnach von wort zů wort zů wort. von stuck zů stucke
armen vnd reichen vngeuerlich richten söllen.

Das ist das rechtbůch also gantz vnd alt gepeffcret.
vnd auch neu artickel gesamlet. auf allen gerichten stett
vnd merckten nach des Kaisers haissen.   ꜰ ɪ

---

except that after 1460 he is believed to have given up printing. However, this may not have been the case, since it is recorded that he received a pension from the Archbishop of Mainz until his death.

Gutenberg's achievement was to invent a system of mass production, enabling books to be produced in greater numbers and more economically. His invention played a fundamental role in the development of the modern world, and was the single most important factor in the spread of knowledge and the move toward universal literacy in the West.

At this time all skills, trades, and professions were guarded jealously by their practitioners, so it is not surprising that there was so much secrecy surrounding Gutenberg's experiments. For centuries a training in printing, as in many other trades, had to be bought through apprenticeship if you were not lucky enough to be born into the family of a printer.

THE ADJUSTABLE MOLD

The brilliance of Gutenberg's invention was in adapting several existing technologies to make them suitable for his own requirements, and, possibly, in using earlier ideas by others such as Coster. Gutenberg's innovations included the modification of the screw press, originally used to crush fruit, and the adaptation of the techniques of punchcutting, brass mold-making, and metal-casting, which were already familiar to silversmiths and engravers. Gutenberg's key innovation was the adjustable mold. This was a

Left: Rotunda. This printed page uses one of the main forms of blackletter, or Gothic Letter, also known as round text.

Below: One of the four main groups that cover vernacular blackletter texts, an example of Bastarda is shown here.

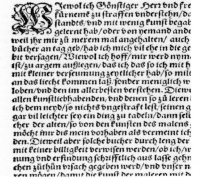

Dem Erberen vnnd wolgeachten ſ
serlicher maiestat raht etc. mein
vnd groserspriesliche
Albrecht Dúre

Iewol ich Gönstiger Herr vnd fre
fürnemé zu straffen vnderstehn/dc
standes vnd mit wenig kunst begabt
gelernt hab/oder von yemand ande
weil jhr mir zů merem mal angehalten/ auch
bücher an tag geb/hab ich mich vil ehe in die ge
bit versagen/Wiewol ich hoff/mir werd nym.
ist/zu argem auslegen/das ich das so ich mit h
mit kleiner verseumung zeytlicher hab/so mit
an das liecht kommen laß sonder meniglich w
loben/vnd den im allerbesten verstehen. Diew
allen kunstliebhabenden/vnd denen so zů leren i
ich dem neyd/so nichts vngestraft lest/seinen g
gar vil leichter sey ein ding zu tadeln/dann self
cher der alten/so von den kunsten des malens.
möcht mir dis mein vorhaben als vermeint ich
den. Dierueil aber solche bücher durch leng der
mit keiner billigkeit verwisen werden/ob ich/v
nung vnd erfindung schrifftlich aus lasse gehn
chen zůthůn vrsach gegeben werd/vnd vnser n
ren mögen/damit die kunst der maleren mit b

Johannes Gutenberg

mechanism of two fitting parts that could be adjusted to fit the matrix of each letter width to be cast, overcoming the problem of the necessity of a mold for each letter. Gutenberg also manufactured a thick, oil-based ink that could achieve a quality of black similar to that of the scribes' inks. His experiments resulted in the inclusion of antimony as part of the metal alloy (mostly lead with some tin) that produced a sharp letter cast from the mold without shrinkage as the metal cooled.

Gutenberg's greatest achievement was the 42-line Bible, completed in about 1455, which imitated the style of the handwritten book to a remarkable degree. His typeface was based on Textura, the formal script of northern Germany. Research suggests that to imitate the inconsistencies and abbreviations that appear in a handwritten manuscript, Gutenberg cast at least 300 characters in order to provide slight variations of letterform throughout the text.

EARLY PUBLICATIONS

There are four main groups of blackletter: Texturas; Gotico-antiquas (or Fere-humanisticas); Rotunda (round text); and Bastards (vernacular types).

In 1462, as the result of a political power struggle, Mainz was subjected to considerable violence and destruction. The resulting desolation and evictions helped to hasten the spread of printing across Europe, as printers became itinerant and were forced to look for new markets.

Right: Printing was brought to the British Isles by William Caxton in 1477. He set up his printing press in the Abbey Precinct at Westminster. His first book in English was printed in Bruges, Belgium, in 1475.

Many ambitious printers would have looked to Italy, the center of the new cultural force that was spreading across Europe—and in particular Venice, hub of international trade, and Rome, the home of the Pope and the center of Western Christianity. For Venice, the invention of printing became yet another opportunity for trade and greater wealth. For the church, mass-produced books that spread ideas not in line with Rome's policies eventually became a grave challenge to its authority.

FROM GOTHIC TO ROMAN

The early years of printing, from Gutenberg's 42-line Bible up to the 1500s, are referred to as the Incunabula Period. In Britain, printing was first introduced by William Caxton (1421–1491). Caxton occupied the post of Governor of English Wool Merchants in Bruges, Belgium. He studied the craft of printing in Germany and printed his first books in English in Bruges in 1475.

In 1476, he returned to England to set up a printing press at the Abbey Precinct, Westminster, "by the sign of the Red Pale." His first book printed in England was *The Dictes and Sayings of the Philosophers* (1477). When he died he had published 73 books in English.

Below: Early printers, like all tradesmen of the time, jealously guarded their craft secrets and practices. This did not, however, stop them from being the subject of artists' engravings.

SERIF MASTERS

3

IN THE LATTER HALF of the 15th century Chancery script was favored by the scribes of the Vatican. It was an expression of the aesthetic philosophy of the Italian Renaissance. In 1455 Conrad Sweynheim and Arnold Pannartz produced a type that demonstrated the first move toward the "White Letter," the lighter, fuller "roman" letterform.

Nicholas Jenson

Five years later, in Venice, two brothers, Johannes and Wendelin da Spira, cut a type that was closer in style to a roman letterform—a 14-point type recognized as an advance on the type designs of Sweynheim and Pannartz. However, it was another newcomer to Italy, Nicholas Jenson (1420 –1480), a Frenchman who settled in Venice in 1468, who was responsible for cutting the first outstanding version of the roman typeface. Cut in 1470, Jenson's Roman had only 23 letters, since "J," "U," and "W" were not yet in use. He

26. *John and Wendelin de Spire's Roman Type, Venice*, 1469
From De Civitate Dei of 1470

Above: Sweynheim and Pannartz working in Subiaco, Italy, in about 1465, cut a typeface for an edition of *Cicero* that was a lighter, fuller form than that of Textura, the formal script of northern Germany.

Left: In Venice, the brothers Johannes and Wendelin da Spira cut a type that was strongly influenced by the humanist hand, itself a rejection of the Gothic form of northern Europe.

used the typeface for an edition of Eusebius's *De Evangelica Praeparatione*. The lowercase alphabet is the same, except that the "v" is used in place of "u," and, in addition, there is a long "s" and "æ" and "œ:" 15 contractions, six double letters, and three full points: 73 punches in all.

FROM A CRAFT TO AN ART

Nicholas Jenson had served an apprenticeship at the Paris Mint, and was promoted to Master of the Mint at Tours. Charles VII sent Jenson to Mainz to learn about the new invention of printing from movable type. He may have met Gutenberg. However, he arrived in Venice and proceeded to set up a printing workshop to print in his own right. At the time of his death in 1480 he had produced about 150 editions.

In 1476, when Jenson produced a volume of Pliny's *Natural History*, he required financial support from the Venetian bankers Strozzi and

Agostini. As a result, payments are recorded of 731 ducats for 86 bales of paper. Each copy was sold for seven ducats. Jenson's type has become renowned for the comfortable fit of the letters as words and the beautiful proportions of the letterforms themselves. The Victorian designer William Morris (1834–1896) was to use Jenson's type as a model for his own Golden Type. The 20th-century typographer Bruce Rogers had a sustained interest in Jenson's roman which culminated in his typeface Centaur, released by Monotype in 1929, and discussed later in this book. In 1996 Robert Slimbach of Adobe designed an excellent digital version of Jenson's roman that is lighter in color than the heavy period quality of Morris's design. Jenson is admired above all other Venetian printers and typecutters of the 15th century because he is considered to have raised type design from a craft to an art form in its own right.

SOME 15 YEARS after Nicholas Jenson's death, another high-quality roman typeface was created in Venice that was to inspire type design for the next century and a half. This was the result of Aldus Manutius's remarkable qualities as a publisher, and the superb skills of his punchcutter, Francesco Griffo of Bologna.

Aldus Manutius

Teobaldo Manuzio, now better known by his Latinized name, Aldus Manutius, studied Greek and Latin in Rome. He developed a love of Greek, believing (in common with many other scholars) that a thorough knowledge of Greek literature was the way to a greater appreciation of the culture and knowledge of antiquity. He was a teacher until, in his forties, he decided that he should attempt the printing and publishing of classical Greek literature in the original language.

When Manutius arrived in Venice in 1489 the market for Latin books was well provided for, but for Greek books there was less demand, since most of Greek literature could already be found in Latin translation. Manutius made contact with writers and scholars. His research rewarded him

with suitable manuscripts to convert into printed books. Venice had had a resident Greek community since the fall of Constantinople in 1453, and members of this community were able to help with the editing and publishing of the texts. Lastly, Manutius needed printers and financial backing. His first book in Venice was a Latin grammar printed by Andrea Torresani in 1493.

EARLY TEXTS

Using the engraving skills of Francesco Griffo (d.1518), it was Manutius's primary intention to produce a satisfactory Greek typeface for his publications. Typographically speaking, ancient Greek had not gone through the process of revision and development in the same way that Latin had. This made it a complex project for type designers.

For their Greek typeface, Manutius and Griffo chose to adapt the calligraphic hand used in Venice at the time, rather than a more formal manuscript hand. Griffo's type influenced subsequent Greek types for many years, although it never received the same acclaim as his roman typefaces. In 1495 the first volume from the Aldine Press, an introduction to Greek grammar, appeared with parallel Latin translation.

Towards the end of the century Manutius turned to Latin editions as well as Greek, since his Greek publications never reached the level of

Left: Venice in the late 15th century was a hive of printing activity. The academic printer Manutius was also a businessman, and was aware that his books should be clearly identified by his device, which showed a dolphin and anchor.

popularity that he had hoped. In 1495, Griffo cut the type used for a Latin text, *De Aetna*, by Pietro Bembo. This was to become the typeface that made the names of Manutius and Griffo part of printing history.

ITALIC TYPE

Manutius added a series of pocket books to his list of publications. This was not a totally original idea, since small books had been produced before. However, for his small-format editions Manutius commissioned Griffo to cut a typeface based on the humanist script that was current—a similar concept to the Greek types he had already cut. Consisting of lowercase only (roman was used for the capital letters), this typeface is what we now call italic. The fact that it was more condensed than a roman face made it more economical in terms of space and thereby reduced the number of pages—an important consideration for cost and weight. These compact volumes of Latin literature were not intended for academics, but for general readers to carry with them to be read when time allowed. They proved to be extremely successful: the first volume, published in 1501, was an edition of *Virgil* which ran to two editions of 3,000 each.

Above: In 1501, Manutius produced the first of his octavo classics, Virgil's *Opera*, which was set entirely in italic type. In this book he praises his typecutter Francesco Griffo.

In the 1600s, the majuscule (uppercase) and miniscule (lowercase) alphabets were viewed as independent components of a roman typeface. The uppercase of a Renaissance italic is often smaller than the uppercase of a roman font of equivalent size, and are, in fact, small caps. During this time, the roman and italic lowercases were kept entirely separate; entire books would be set in roman or italic but never mixed both. Consequently, authors of modern Old-style revivals have had to artificially match these independent designs.

Manutius guarded his publications and types jealously and claimed copyright and monopolies from the College of Venice. This resulted in a dispute with Francesco Griffo as to the true authorship of the Aldine set of types. Griffo claimed that he had not been given enough credit for his part in their creation and was restrained legally from cutting further types in the same style, reducing his ability to trade.

DURING THE 16TH CENTURY, French printing gained prominence over that of Italy. The middle years of the century have been called the Golden Age of French book arts.

Claude Garamond

Some of the important printers of this period were Simon de Colines, Jean de Tournes, Robert Estienne (son of Henri, the father of the dynasty of printer/publishers), and Geoffroy Tory, whose skills and learning were rewarded by promotion to become the first Imprimeur de Roi, the king's printer. This was a period when the printer still took responsibility for deciding what to print, so that printer/publishers were well-educated in the classics of Greek and Latin literature as well as in their native language.

Garamond had been apprenticed to Antoine Augereau, a Protestant printer/scholar who, like Geoffroy Tory, had been instrumental in promoting the use of the humanist Aldine roman types rather than the Gothic blackletter, which still maintained favor with some French printers.

In Paris, Garamond worked for several printers at first, but was taken up by his contemporary Robert Estienne, when Estienne commissioned a set of punches from the ambitious young punchcutter. Eventually, in 1526, Robert took over the running of the press from his stepfather and became the royal printer of Hebrew, Latin, and Greek.

Garamond took the opportunity to become independent, and established himself as the leading French typecutter. The new roman that Garamond cut was used in Estienne's edition of *Pharaphrasis in Elegantiarium* by Erasmus, which appeared, together with several other publications in the series, in 1530.

A HARMONIOUS SET

There is little doubt that Garamond gained inspiration from Francesco Griffo for his own designs. However, Garamond introduced refinements to the Old-face which he maintained and modified over the years.

The italics that Griffo had cut for Manutius were only lowercase letters. Garamond took up the idea to cut a companion italic alphabet, with italic capitals that would partner roman fonts, a concept that is now a basic feature of all text faces. The combination and balance of capitals with a lowercase and italic alphabet provided the printer with a comprehensive and harmonious set of letterforms for the first time.

The success of Garamond's types results from their technical brilliance as well as from the quality of the design. His ambition to set up independently and make full use of his skills and connections helped to establish the cutting and casting of type as a specialized skill separate from printing.

After the death of Claude Garamond in 1561, his punches and matrices were sold. The biggest collection was purchased by Christopher Plantin, the French printer/publisher based in Antwerp.

Left: A 16th-century title page showing Garamond's types in use, including small capitals and italics with swash capitals, surrounded by an elaborate border composed of columns and foliage.

K

K

Above: The uppercase letters of Garamond (top) show greater contrast of stroke thickness compared Bembo (above). Note the subtle swelling of the rising arm of the "K," as it meets the serif. Garamond's Roman has a lighter color on the page. The serifs, while larger, have smaller bracketing than the more austere Aldine Roman.

AFTER THE DEATH of Claude Garamond, a large quantity of his punches and matrices were purchased by printer and publisher Christopher Plantin. Plantin was also French, born near Tours in 1520. He had trained and worked as a bookbinder, spending a number of years in Paris and traveling around France.

Christopher Plantin

Plantin settled in Antwerp, which was at the time under the rule of the Spanish Habsburgs. After an injury that affected his ability to work as a bookbinder, he turned to printing and publishing in 1555. He quickly gathered around him a group of scholars, linguists, and theologians, and proceeded to publish a wide range of scholarly volumes. Although produced in the Netherlands, Plantin's publications were still effectively French. Not only had he been trained in France, but from the start he acquired much of his equipment, materials, and types from France.

Plantin is said to have had as many as 21 presses operating in his workshop when at full capacity, with a team of men to each press, each man carrying out his allotted function: one inking the type, one feeding paper in, one operating the lever to pull the impression, one removing the printed sheet.

Apart from his collection of the acclaimed Garamond types, Plantin was successful enough in his publishing enterprise to be able to commission types from other typefounders, in particular Robert Granjon of Lyon, who was also

Left: A general view of part of the Plantin-Moretus Museum of Printing in Antwerp, once the press room of the Plantin publishing house. The heavy wooden presses on the left are fitted with struts from the ceiling. These steadied the presses as the continuous pulling action of the pressmen meant they were likely to move.

REGNI NEAPOLITANI
PRIVILEGIVM.

PHILIPPVS DEI GRATIA REX
CASTELLÆ, ARAGONVM, VTRIVSQVE
SICILIÆ, HIERVSALEM, VNGARIÆ, DALMATIÆ, ET CROATIÆ, &c.

NTONIVS Perrenotus, S.R.C.tit. Sancti Petri ad Vincula Presby-
ter, Cardinalis de Granuela, præfatæ Regiæ & Catholicæ Maiestatis
à consiliis status, & in hoc Regno locum tenens, & Capitaneus ge-
neralis, &c. Mag.co viro Christophoro Plantino, ciui Antuerpien-
si, & præfatæ Catholicæ Maiestatis Prototypographo fideli Re-
gio, dilecto, gratiam Regiam & bonam voluntatem. Cùm ex præ-
clarorum virorum literis certiores facti simus, opus Bibliorum quinque linguarum,
cum tribus Apparatuum tomis, celeberrimum, reíque publicæ Christianæ vtilissimú,
eiusdem serenissimæ Maiestatis iussu, ope atque auspiciis, ad publicam totius Chri-
stiani orbis commoditatem & ornamentum, typis longè elegantissimis, & præstan-
tissimi viri Benedicti Ariæ Montani præcipua cura & studio. quàm emendatissimè
à te excusum esse, eiusdemq́; exemplar sanctissimo Domino nostro PP. Gregorio XIII.
oblatum, ita plàcuisse, vt præfatæ Maiestatis sanctos conatus, & Regi Catholico in
primis conuenientes, summopere laudarit, & amplissima tibi priuilegia ad hoc opus
tuendum Motu proprio concesserit; Nos quoque cum naturali genio impellimur ad
fouendum præclara quæque ingenia, quæ insigni quopiam conatu ad publica com-

resident in Antwerp for a period. Granjon provided several of Plantin's civilité types (a cursive
type based on the hand of the period, which
could be described as a kind of French italic) and
the Greek and Syriac for Plantin's master work,
the *Polyglot Bible*. The *Polyglot Bible* was a massive eight-volume production, including texts in
Hebrew, Greek, Latin, Chaldaic, and Syriac, produced between 1569 and 1572 under the patronage
of King Philip II of Spain.

The typecutter Hendrik van den Keere started
working for Plantin in 1568 and from 1570 was
responsible for the typefoundry work and 40 sets
of punches and matrices, which are still with the
Plantin-Moretus Museum in Antwerp to this day.

DUTCH RISE TO PROMINENCE

After Plantin's death in 1589, his son-in-law
Johannes Moretus continued to run the business,
and was succeeded by his son Balathasar.

The prominence of French printing gave way
to the Netherlands largely through the efforts of
the Plantin-Moretus dynasty and later, in the 17th
century, the Elzevir dynasty. There was also a
demand in continental Europe and Britain for the
work of a number of remarkable Netherlands
typecutters: van den Keere, Christoffel van Dyck,
and Dirck Voskens.

The Plantin typeface issued by Monotype in
1913, although named after the printer, was
based on a Robert Granjon type used by Plantin's
successors. This was found in use in Frankfurt,
Germany, and Basle, Switzerland, at the end of
the 16th century.

Plantin is a stocky face compared with most
Old-faces, with a large x-height. The current
digital range of Plantin includes a light as well
as roman. There is also semibold as well as
bold, all with accompanying italics, plus a single
bold condensed.

WILLIAM CASLON (1692–1766) was the father of British typography and his work is the typographic embodiment of the English Baroque.

William Caslon

In 1586, the Archbishop of Canterbury and the Bishop of London were empowered by the Privy Council to control the number of printing presses in Oxford, Cambridge, and London; printing was not allowed elsewhere in England. The restrictions on the number of printing presses and therefore the size of the industry had a damaging effect: the quality of printed work declined, and English printers became dependent on types imported from the Netherlands, either as metal type or as matrices to be cast locally. These restrictions were lifted during the mid-17th century, although censorship remained in place. In the 1670s, however, when Dr John Fell and his committee set about improving print quality at Oxford University, it was still necessary for him to buy a collection of types and punches from Holland for the university's press to use. Due to these restrictions it was natural that William Caslon chose the Dutch Old-face as his model when cutting his first English Old-face types.

CRAFTSMAN AND INNOVATOR

Caslon has been called the greatest British type-cutter and founder. The establishment of his type-foundry was a landmark in English printing because, with the quality of his types, he was able (almost single-handedly) to eliminate the need for imported Dutch types.

Above: Caslon Foundry specimen sheet. Caslon was the first internationally known British typefounder. The Caslon Foundry's type specimen sheet (above) did not appear until some ten years after he established his typefoundry.

Born in 1692, Caslon started his working life as an engraver. He set himself up in business engraving hunting guns and cutting punches for bookbinders' tooling. His fine work brought him to the attention of the printers John Watts and William Bowyer, who were impressed with the quality of Caslon's skills—so much so that they offered Caslon financial support to set up a typefoundry. In the same year of 1720, as a result of Caslon's growing reputation, the Society for the Promotion of Christian Knowledge used Caslon in a Psalter in 1725 and a New Testament in 1727, for its overseas mission. At the foot of Caslon's proofs for this font, he added his name cut in a pica roman. Bowyer was so impressed by these few letters that he encouraged Caslon to cut a complete roman font in that style. As a result, Caslon produced a roman and italic font, as well as one of Hebrew that was used by Bowyer for a folio edition, published in 1726.

Caslon cut several other faces required by his patron, Bowyer, including Coptic and other exotic types. It was possibly due to the intensity of his workload that he did not issue a specimen sheet of his types until 1734, 14 years after opening the typefoundry for business.

His designs soon achieved acceptance by many of the major printing houses, including King George's printer, who used his types to the exclusion of others. Caslon's reputation also spread abroad, but his English types marked the end of the historical Old-face. On the European continent the turn of the century had brought about changes in type aesthetics, and by the mid-century in Birmingham, England, John Baskerville was exploring new forms.

Caslon died at 74 in 1766, and the business was continued by his son, William Caslon II. Also an excellent craftsman he maintained his father's standards, expanding the company further. The Caslon Foundry continued until 1937, when it became part of the Sheffield Foundry, Stephenson, Blake, & Company, which was to become Britain's last metal typefoundry.

Right: In laying the foundations of modern science, Newton (1643–1727) was a major influence during the enlightenment and beyond. He defined gravity, and discovered that white light is composed of the color spectrum. The form of his *Philosophiae Naturalis Principia Mathematica* (1687), is typical of the publications to appear throughout the enlightenment.

abcdefghijklnopqrst

ABCDEFGHIJKLM

abcdefghijklmnopqrst

Caslon's first roman rapidly became a success when it appeared in the 1720s. This was largely because it was the first opportunity British printers had to use an unrivaled British typeface instead of those imported from Holland. It is a typeface that has a uniquely friendly individuality, with many quirks and inconsistencies, making it remarkably readable; it has endeared itself to generations of English-speaking printers, publishers, and readers. Indeed, the leading English dramatist George Bernard Shaw insisted that all his books were printed in Caslon. In its stocky geometry, freehand curves, and modest baseline serifs, it maintains the practical qualities that made the Dutch types so popular. The lower-case at the x-height have wedge-shaped serifs on "i," "j," "m," "n," and "r," but not on the "u," which has a lighter serif, square to the x-height. The distinct contrast of thick and hairline strokes can seem uneven when examined on individual letters, but strangely, when set in words, this works well.

Caslon became established in the 18th century and spread over the English-speaking world as part of the instruments of colonial rule. When it was first printed in 1776 by John Dunlap, the American Declaration of Independence was typeset in a Caslon type exported to the United States. Caslon's popularity faded for a while at the end of the 18th century because of competition from a new style of face, the transitional, led by Baskerville and Fournier. But in the mid-19th century there was a revival of interest in the Oldface, and it appeared again in the specimen books in 1857. Almost simultaneously, there was a revival in the United States when it was issued by the Philadelphia Foundry of L. J. Johnston.

20TH-CENTURY CASLON

The popularity of Caslon Old-face is evident from the number of versions available throughout the 20th century. The original Caslon was available from Stephenson, Blake, & Company for hand-setting as recently as 2001. There were two hot metal Caslons: Monotype cut a version in 1915 and Linotype cut one in 1921. The ATF Caslon 540 (1905) was an adaption of the Johnston Caslon.

DIGITAL CASLON

There are at least nine digital versions of Caslon available. Most supply a full range of sizes, but Adobe Caslon, designed by Carol Twombly in 1990 and consisting of 20 variants including swash capitals with the italics, is suitable only for text

uvwxyz&1234567890

NOPQRSTUVWXYZ

uvwxyz&1234567890

Above: The 1905 ATF version, Caslon 540, derived from the Johnston adaption. It includes probably the most iconic character in typographic history, the Caslon italic ampersand.

setting, since the design has modified Caslon's original characteristics by reducing the contrasts and increasing the weight of the serifs. It functions well in smaller sizes, but the loss of the unique Caslon character is very noticeable in display sizes. Matthew Carter's Big Caslon is a crisp, geometrically refined design that expresses the contrasting stroke thickness of Caslon with elegance, designed specifically for display work. ITC Caslon, digitized by Justin Howes, released in 1998 consists of four versions of Caslon, that closely follows Caslon's original metal designs. This is a range for the Caslon connoisseur and is an attempt at following the founder's traditional practice of making modifications to letterforms by way of optical corrections to suit a particular size. Founders 12 is for text based on a pica Caslon,

and has noticeably uneven edges and more irregularities than the larger display sizes. Founders 30 is based on two-line English Caslon and 42 on a two-line double pica Caslon. Following 18th-century conventions, there are no bolds, and figures are Old-style (like lowercase, they align with the x-height); there are italics and small capitals. ITC also has a Caslon range designed in 1982 by Edward Benguiat. Caslon Classico, designed by Franko Luin in 1993 and available from Linotype, is a modest range of roman and bold, italics, and roman small capitals. Berthold offer two ranges of Caslon: Caslon 471 in regular, and italics, and Caslon Book in regular, medium, and bold with expert fonts.

nr u

Caslon's types were a great achievement but the last of a line of Old-faces. These three lowercase letters set in Adobe Caslon show the heavier, triangular serif on the "w" and "r" not applied to the "u."

THE TRANSITION

WILLIAM CASLON'S TYPEFACES met with success in Britain, but they were based on the types of the 16th century. As Caslon's typefoundry expanded, almost simultaneously there was a development in France that moved type design into a new age; this was the first of the transitional typefaces.

In 1692, Louis XIV of France commissioned a new collection of types to be created for the exclusive use of the *Imprimerie Royale* under the leadership of Jacques Jaugeon.

The formation of a committee to consider the requirements of a typeface was a break with the traditions of past centuries. These were the early years of the new scientific age, and the committee studied a considerable quantity of writing on letterforms and type from previous generations, including those of Albrect Dürer and Geofroy Tory, as well as contemporary writing masters. The results of their deliberations were drawn using a grid of 2,304 small squares, to determine the proportions of each letter. A series of copper plates engraved with the final letters was executed between 1695 and 1718 as the committee's work proceeded slowly. The calligraphic flow, or the forms echoing the movement of the broad pen, was no longer evident: these forms were determined by mathematics rather than craft.

The first cutting of the punches was entrusted to Philippe Grandjean de Fouchy, a typecutter with a growing reputation, and his assistant Jean Alexandre. Grandjean and Jaugeon seem to have had disagreements from time to time during this period, because Grandjean was not altogether convinced by the mathematical certainty of the forms as presented on the copper plates. This point of friction and other revisions resulted in punches being destroyed and others remade.

Among the issues tackled by the committee was the rationalizing of type body sizes. A system was devised to standardize a unit of type measurement based on the *pied du roi*, the unit of linear measurement at the time. This system made it possible to establish collections of types with interrelated body sizes—an important rationalization for letterpress printing, which was not fully implemented in France until 1775.

Right: *Romain du Roi* (King's Roman), consisted of 21 sizes of roman and italics, and 21 roman and italic initial letters—a total of 84 fonts. The serif brackets are less prominent than on Old-face types. Ascenders are designed with serifs on both sides at the head of the stem, adding horizontal emphasis. The contrast between thick and thin strokes is more pronounced compared to the types of Garamond and his school, and the overall appearance is of a lighter weight than Old-face.

Far right: The King's Roman Grandjean's types for the French King Louis XIV, were first used in 1702, although the complete range was not finished until 1745.

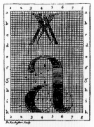

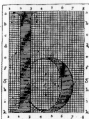

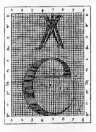

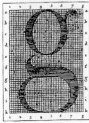

AUTRE MEDAILLE
SUR LA NAISSANCE DU ROY.

COMME les Romains ont eû soin de frapper des Médailles, pour perpétuer dans tous les siécles le souvenir de la constellation, sous laquelle l'Empereur Auguste estoit né ; on a voulu de mesme, sans rien donner aux chiméres de l'Astrologie, transmettre à la postérité la mémoire de la position, où se trouvoit le Ciel dans le moment que Dieu donna à la France le Prince, qui la rend la plus florissante Monarchie du monde.

C'est le sujet de cette Médaille. On a placé tout au tour les douze Signes, & les sept Planetes, dans la mesme position, où ils estoient au moment de cette heureuse naissance ; & suivant l'idée de la Devise du Roy, dont le Soleil est le corps, on a représenté au milieu la naissance de ce Prince, par la figure du Soleil, qui se leve. Le Roy enfant est assis sur un Char élevé au dessus des nuës, & tiré par quatre chevaux. Le Char est mené par la Victoire, qui d'une main luy montre une Couronne de laurier, symbole des avantages, qu'il doit remporter sur les Ennemis de la France ; & qui de l'autre main tient les guides de ses Chevaux, comme pour l'asseurer qu'elle le conduira dans toutes ses entreprises. Les mots de la Légende, ORTUS SOLIS GALLICI, signifient, *le lever du Soleil de la France.* Ceux de l'Exergue, SEPTEMBRIS QUINTO, MINUTIS TRIGINTA OCTO ANTE MERIDIEM. M. DC. XXXVIII. veulent dire, *le Roy né le 5 de Septembre, trente-huit minutes avant midy 1638.*

THE NEW *ROMAIN DU ROI* had many admirers, among them the typefounder Pierre Simon Fournier. He later claimed that his business was the first in France to carry out every aspect of typefounding: designing, cutting punches, striking matrices, making molds, and casting type.

The point system

Unlike his contemporary Caslon, Fournier was born into a family of typefounders and printers. His father Jean-Claude had been the manager of the Paris typefoundry LeBé for almost 30 years. His older brother Jean-Pierre Fournier (1706–1783), known as "the elder," was a typecutter and founder who bought the LeBé in 1730. His second brother François was a printer in Auxerre, the birthplace of his father.

Pierre Simon Fournier had studied drawing as a child, which was most likely the beginning of his attraction to letterforms. At first he worked for his older brother at the typefoundry, and as he gained experience he was allowed to engrave punches for capital letters (large initial letters normally cut from wood). In 1736 Fournier set up in business in his own right. He quickly gained a reputation for his technical brilliance as a typecutter and founder, and for the technical innovations he introduced. As a type designer he was not an innovator; his ability lay in the adaption and developments he made to the ideas of others. This accounts for his appreciation of the *Romain du Roi* types, which he emulated despite the king's prohibition.

MEASUREMENT SYSTEM

In 1737, Fournier began to formulate a system of comparative type body sizes. The typeface body

sizes of early typefounders were not standardized; founders cast their type on bodies of their own specification. Any given typeface was generally only cut in a limited number of sizes. Names were used to give an indication of size, some were derived from a historic publication in which the type of that size had first been used: for example, Cicero, the continental 12-point, is said to originate from Fust & Schoeffer's edition of Cicero's *De Oratore*, printed in a type close to 12 Didot points in about 1466. Other examples are Brevier, a size between 7.7- and 7.9-point, and Great Primer, a size between 16.6- and 16.9-point.

Fournier based his standard on two inches; each inch divided up into 12 lines and each line into six typographic points, making 144 typographic points overall. Therefore two *nonpareils* (a *nonpareil* being equivalent to six points) equals one Cicero. This offered a measurement system that was of great practical benefit, although it was not taken up by other foundries for another decade or so.

Fournier's most remarkable achievement, and the culmination of many years dedicated to the perfection of his art of typography, was his two-volume *Manuel Typographique*. The preface to the first volume, published in 1764, was set in his remarkable italics. The following pages contained example after example of types set in an elegant display of the typography of the period, many borrowed from his brother's typefoundry collection, including a number of large, simple initial letters not commonly available. Also displayed, with great elegance and refinement, were a large variety of typographic ornaments modified to the taste of the day. These were intended to replace the copperplate engravings used by many printers.

Fournier's two-volume set explained the mysteries of the practice and art of typefounding and was the most authoritative publication available at the time. Volume II appeared in 1766, two years before he died (from what some have described as overwork). In a span of 28 years he had cut over 80 fonts of type, as well as managing the daily work of the typefoundry.

Soutien du Temple de mémoire,
Nous transmettons les Faits à la postérité,
Les Arts, les Sciences, l'Histoire
Nous doivent l'Immortalité.

TABLE GÉNÉRALE
DE LA PROPORTION
des différens Corps de Caractères.

ÉCHELLE FIXE
de 144 points Typographiques.

Nomb.	Corps.	Points
1	PARISIENNE.	5
2	NOMPAREILLE.	6
3	MIGNONE.	7
4	PETIT-TEXTE.	8
5	GAILLARDE. . . . , ...	9
6	PETIT-ROMAIN. – 2 Parisiennes.	10
7	PHILOSOPHIE. = 1 Parif. 1 Nompareille.	11
8	CICÉRO. – 2 Nomp. = 1 Parisienne, 1 Mignone.	12
9	SAINT-AUGUSTIN. – 2 Mignones. = 1 Nompareille, 1 Petit-texte.	14

Above: A heavenly typefoundry. This engraved frontispiece is from the second volume of Fournier's *Manule Typographique*, printed in 1766.

Above: Fournier spent many years devising a system of interrelated type sizes, which he put into practice in his own typefoundry. The chart explained his ideas.

DURING HIS LIFETIME John Baskerville was considered something of an eccentric, and in Britan his ideas on type design were not met with much enthusiasm initially. Some critics even suggested that his type was bad for the eyes. However, in continental Europe his innovations were received with greater appreciation.

John Baskerville

John Baskerville was born in Worcestershire, England in 1706 and moved to Birmingham at the age of 19, where he trained as a writing master and stone engraver. After some years, he was able to invest in the manufacture of "Japanned Goods," which utilized a method of varnishing furniture, screens, and smaller items such as tea trays and snuff boxes to achieve a hard, brilliant finish.

Baskerville found success in this very lucrative activity and after a number years achieved financial security, becoming a established figure in Birmingham. In 1750, his achievements allowed him to turn his attention to printing, and he set up a printing press at the age of 44.

Baskerville's typeface, cut by his employee John Handy, was completed after many false starts owing to Baskerville's perfectionism. The complete set of punches took approximately three years to complete. His first book, and edition of classic poetry by Virgil, appeared in 1757. In his striving for perfection Baskerville explored ways of improving the printing press, to make it capable of greater precision, more subtle impressions, and the printing of more delicate types. He also devised improvements in the quality of his printing ink. He had paper woven to his specification, he developed a method of further smoothing the paper, and he lent a

brilliance to type by passing the printed sheets between heated copper plates. With this attention to detail Baskerville was able to produce books of great elegance.

BASKERVILLE'S LEGACY

Baskerville's perfectionism tended to hinder his financial success. Shortly before he died he tried to sell the printing press and his punches, without success. After he died, his widow maintained the business for a while, but eventually sold the complete Baskerville typefoundry to the French Pierre Augustin Caron de Beaumachais in 1779. Beaumachais was a playwright, secret agent, and visitor to the London house of John Wilkes (a friend of Baskerville). He was also a friend of Benjamin Franklin and supporter of American independence from the British king. He acquired the contents of the Baskerville typefoundry with the intention of printing the collected works of the French enlightenment philosopher, Voltaire, whose work was prohibited in France. Beaumachais was also the author of *The Barber of Seville* and *The Marriage of Figaro*, better known today as the 18th-century operas by Rossini and Mozart respectively. The surviving 2,750 punches from Baskerville's original collection was presented to Cambridge University Press in England, in 1953.

THE

P S A L T E R,

OR

P S A L M S of D A V I D,

Pointed as they are to be fung or faid in Churches.

THE FIRST DAY.
MORNING PRAYER.

PSAL. I. *Beatus vir, qui non abiit.*

BLESSED is the man that hath not walked
in the counfel of the ungodly, nor flood
in the way of finners: and hath not fat in the
feat of the fcornful.

2 But his delight is in the law of the Lord:
and in his law will he exercife himfelf day and
night.

3 And he fhall be like a tree planted by the
water-fide: that will bring forth his fruit in
due feafon.

4 His leaf alfo fhall not wither: and look,
whatfoever he doeth, it fhall profper.

5 As for the ungodly, it is not fo with them:
but they are like the chaff which the wind
fcattereth away from the face of the earth.

6 Therefore the ungodly fhall not be able
to fland in the judgment: neither the finners
in the congregation of the righteous.

7 But

THE

CONTAINING THE

OLD TESTAMENT

AND

THE NEW:

Tranflated out of the

AND

With the former TRANSLATIONS

Diligently Compared and Revifed,

By His MAJESTY's Special Command.

APPOINTED TO BE READ IN CHURCHES.

C A M B R I D G E.

Printed by *JOHN BASKERVILLE,* Printer to the UNIVERSITY.
M DCC LXIII.

CUM PRIVILEGIO

Above and above right:
Baskerville achieved one of
his dearest wishes in 1758:
the opportunity to print bibles
and prayer books for the
Cambridge University Press.

Right: Baskerville's typography
was influenced by a revival of
interest in the classical. His page
layout has a pure simplicity,
with letter-spaced capitals
and generous margins. Such
simplicity needs great attention
to the details of proportion.

P. VIRGILII MARONIS

AENEIDOS

LIBER SEXTUS.

SIc fatur lacrymans: clafsique immittit habenas.
Et tandem Euboicis Cumarum allabitur oris.
Obvertunt pelago proras: tum dente tenaci
Ancora fundabat naves, et litora curvæ
5 Prætexunt puppes. juvenum manus emicat ardens
Litus in Hefperium: quærit pars femina flammæ
Abftrufa in venis filicis: pars denfa ferarum
Tecta rapit, filvas: inventaque flumina monftrat.
At pius Aeneas arces, quibus altus Apollo
10 Præfidet, horrendæque procul fecreta Sibyllæ
Antrum immane, petit: magnam cui mentem animumque
Delius infpirat vates, aperitque futura.
Jam fubeunt Triviæ lucos, atque aurea tecta.
Dædalus, ut fama eft, fugiens Minoïa regna,
15 Præpetibus pennis aufus fe credere cælo,
Infuetum per iter geliäas enavit ad Arctos,
Chalcidicäque levis tandem fuperaftitit arce.
Redditus his primum terris, tibi, Phœbe, facravit
Remigium alarum: pofuitque immania templa.
20 In foribus lethum Androgeo: tum pendere pœnas
Cecropidæ

P. VIRGILII AENEIDOS LIB. VI. 255

Cecropidæ jufsi (miferum!) feptena quotannis
Corpora natorum. ftat ductis fortibus urna.
Contra elata mari refpondet Gnofia tellus:
Hic crudelis amor tauri, fuppoftaque furto
25 Pafiphaë, nictumque genus, prolefque biformis
Minotaurus ineft, Veneris monumenta nefandæ.
Hic labor ille domus, et inextricabilis error.
Magnum Reginæ fed enim miferatus amorem
Dædalus, ipfe dolos tecti, ambagefque refolvit,
30 Cæca regens filo veftigia. tu quoque magnam
Partem opere in tanto, fineret dolor, Icare, haberes.
Bis conatus erat cafus effingere in auro:
Bis patriæ cecidere manus. quin protinus omnia
Perlegerent oculis: ni jam præmiffus Achates
35 Afforet, atque una Phœbi Triviæque facerdos,
Deiphobe Glauci: fatur quæ talia Regi:
Non hoc illa fibi tempus fpectacula pofcit.
Nunc grege de intacto feptem mactare juvencos
Præftiterit, totidem lectas de more bidentes.
40 Talibus affata Aeneas (nec fuera morantur
Jufsa viri) Teucros vocat alta in templa facerdos.
Excifum Euboicæ latus ingens rupis in antrum:
Quo lati ducunt aditus centum, oftia centum.
Unde ruunt totidem voces, refponfa Sibyllæ.
45 Ventum erat ad limen, quum Virgo, Pofcere fata
Tempus, ait. Deus, ecce, Deus. Cui talia fanti
Ante fores, fubito non vultus, non color unus,
Non comtæ manfere comæ: fed pectus anhelum,
Et rabie fera corda tument: majorque videri,
50 Nec mortale fonans: afflata eft numine quando
Jam propiore Dei. Cefsas in vota precefque

G g 2 Tros,

FRANÇOIS DIDOT (1689–1757), was the patriarch of a family of remarkable printers, publishers, typecutters, and papermakers, and with his sons, François Ambroise and Pierre, made significant contributions to the development of French printing.

The Didot dynasty

3

François Ambroise Didot (1730–1804) introduced France to the fine-surfaced paper favored by Baskerville. He was commissioned in 1783 by Louis XVI to produce an elegant collection of classical French authors. The types were cut by his former apprentice Pierre-Louis Vaflard to François Ambroise's specification, which expressed the classical mode.

François Ambroise established the Didot point system, the type body-sizing method that had first been contemplated by the *Académie des Sciences* in the 1690s and developed subsequently by Fournier. François Ambroise standardized the point at 72 points to the French inch, and with royal authority Didot's rationalization became the accepted standard in France by the end of the century. When the metric system was introduced by Napoleon in 1801, however, Didot tried to adapt his system, without success—another change so soon was unacceptable to printers and foundries. When the grandson of Benjamin Franklin, the American scientist and diplomat, wished to take up an apprenticeship in printing, it was François Ambroise that Franklin recommended he contact.

A FAMILY BUSINESS

François Ambroise's two sons, Pierre and Firmin, both continued the family business. Pierre took over the running of the printing office and Firmin distinguished himself as a typefounder. While still working for his father in 1784, he cut punches for a letterform that have since been claimed to be the first Modern type. His design reduced serifs and the thin strokes to fine lines, and increased the contrast of the thick strokes.

Firmin printed his work on smooth-surfaced, woven paper, which was made possible through improvements in the presswork. Firmin's father proudly used his son's typographic creations for

Left: The engraving shows the typecasting machine invented by Henri Didot, son of Pierre François Didot. It was taken over by his nephew Marcellini Legrand and patented in 1829. One of these machines was taken to London by the typefounder Louis Pouchée a few years later.

a fine edition of the Renaissance poet Tasso's *Gerusalemme Liberta*.

Pierre's printing and publishing skills were admired greatly, so much so that his printing office was allocated premises in the Louvre. From this location, he produced a series of elegantly illustrated volumes of French and Latin classics known as *Editions du Louvre*. In 1818 he bought, from the Beaumarchais family, the sets of punches for 22 Baskerville types.

Firmin's two sons, Ambroise Firmin and his brother Hyacinthe, maintained the publishing side of the family firm as Firmin Didot Brothers into the 19th century. Pierre's son Henri was

highly regarded for his cutting of microscopic types. His brother Saint-Léger, a paper manufacturer, was responsible for supporting the early developments of a papermaking machine, later perfected in England.

Firmin Didot gained great prominence for the quality of his types and they represented the cool elegance of the neoclassical age in France. He was also an inspiration to others, particularly the great genius of the Modern letterform, the Italian printer Giambattista Bodoni. Didot was made director of the typefoundry of the *Imprimerie Impériale* by Napoleon, and died in 1836 having received many honors.

QUINTI

HORATII FLACCI

CARMINUM

LIBER QUARTUS.

ODE I.

AD VENEREM.

Intermissa, Venus, diu
Rursus bella moves. Parce, precor, precor!
Non sum qualis eram bonæ
Sub regno Cinaræ. Desine, dulcium
Mater sæva Cupidinum,
Circa lustra decem flectere mollibus
Iam durum imperiis. Abi
Quo blandæ iuvenum te revocant preces.

*167. Page of folio Horace: Pierre Didot, Paris, 1799
(reduced)*

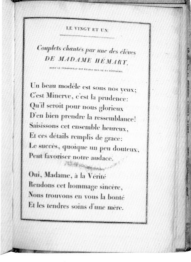

Left: A page from Pierre Didot's 1799 edition of Horace, the Roman poet. A fine example of the vertically stressed French Modern type style.

Above: A page from Didot's prospectus showing his version of the Modern Roman; this was to become the style of the 19th-century text face.

THE BRILLIANT PRINTER and punchcutter who, more than anyone, brought the Modern face to the height of elegance and sophistication was the Italian, Giambattista Bodoni. The typeface reached a peak of perfection in the late 18th century, although as a style it remained popular throughout the 19th century.

Giambattista Bodoni

By the end of the 18th century Modern itself had come under attack, being described as an adulterated construct that was lacking the qualities for good legibility, and so began its fall from favor. However, the Modern letterform at the close of the 18th century was one created by the aesthetics and technical refinements of a new Classical age, far from the calligraphically-derived forms of the Renaissance.

Bodoni was born in Saluzzo, northern Italy, in 1740. He was the son of a printer, so he came into contact with printing at an early age, and soon picked up skill in the practice of engraving woodblocks. At the age of 18, he became a compositor in the Vatican Printing Office in Rome. He was ambitious and quick to learn, and having shown an interest in Oriental languages, he was put in charge of the Vatican Oriental typefaces. Many of these had been cut some two centuries earlier by such names as Garamond and Grandjean, and they now required organizing and cataloging, since they were in a bad state of neglect. It was this experience that broadened Bodoni's interest in letterforms, at times designing and cutting typographic ornaments for use in the department.

FROM CRAFTSMAN TO ARTIST

John Baskerville's reputation and printing achievements had reached Italy, and in 1768, at the age of 28, Bodoni decided that he should travel to England and meet Baskerville for himself. However, when preparing for his journey to Birmingham in Britain, he fell sick with malaria and was forced to spend time recovering at his family home in Saluzzo. It was while convalescing that he received a proposal from the Duke of Parma, who had learned of Bodoni from contacts at the Vatican.

The Duke was the patron of a library and academy of art in Parma, and he was planning to increase his prestige by setting up a printing office with the intention of printing fine books. He asked Bodoni to become the director, which Bodoni was keen to do. He started work at the Stamperia Reale, Parma, in 1768, and would spend the rest of his working life there. The first types he chose to print with were the transitional types of Pierre Simon Fournier. However, Bodoni was ambitious, and soon designed his own types that fully expressed his concept of elegance. These were demonstrated in his specimen book, prepared in 1771.

GIAMBATTISTA BODONI

A CHI LEGGE.

Eccovi i saggi dell'industria e delle fatiche mie di molti anni consecrati con veramente geniale impegno ad un'arte, che è compimento della più bella, ingegnosa, e giovevole invenzione degli uomini, voglio dire dello scrivere, di cui è la stampa la miglior maniera, ogni qual volta sia pregio dell'opera far a molti copia delle stesse parole, e maggiormente quando importi aver certezza che

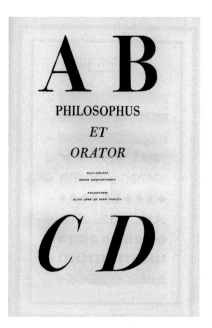

PHILOSOPHUS
ET
ORATOR

fonderia: il Manuale presente ne renderà esatto conto, qualora vogliasi confrontare col primo. Converrammi piuttosto osservare, che il sesto e il contorno sono i medesimi ch'egli vivente diede ad alcune pagine fatte imprimere per prova. In queste, a differenza del suo primo Manuale, ove ogni pagina conteneva la descrizione di una qualche città, comincian-

Top left and left: The *Manuale Tipografico*, Bodoni's master work, which contained specimens of his enormous collection of types and his views on the art of type design, printed in 1788. The second volume was published posthumously by his wife in 1818, five years after his death.

Above: Another page from the the *Manuale Tipografico* showing the use of the largest and smallest of Bodoni's collection of roman and italic capitals.

DISPLAY TYPE

BY THE EARLY 19TH CENTURY typefoundries had a new kind of client, demanding a new sort of typeface. The new client was the jobbing printer, and his demand was for "display" typefaces. The jobbing printer's role emerged from increasingly sophisticated commercial activity and its accompanying need for publicity materials.

Type gets bigger and bolder

In towns and cities the advertising needs of all kinds of businesses, ranging from patent medicine vendors to auctioneers, were served by the local jobbing printer.

Large poster types were needed. The large decorated and engraved letters that were in existence in the 18th century, especially those of Pierre Simon Fournier, were only intended for the title pages of books. The manufacture of display types was an area of enterprise that gave British typefoundries an opportunity to develop their range of typefaces.

The first design to successfully fulfil the requirements of display type became known as the "fat-face," the invention of which is credited

to Robert Thorne (1754–1820). Thorne's simple but ingenious concept was to make use of the vogue for the continental Modern face, such as Bodoni. By increasing the thickness of the stems to an enormous degree, while maintaining the thin strokes and the thin, unbracketed serifs, he produced a fierce blackletter of enormous power. It was extremely popular with advertisers, but filled many typographic commentators with horror. Nonetheless, the idea soon gained favor with other foundries and their customers.

Robert Thorne, one of the outstanding typefounders of the 19th century, had been apprentice to Thomas Cottrell. After Cottrell's death, Thorne bought the typefoundry and its collection of

DOUBLE PICA No. 2.

How far, O Catiline, wilt thou abuse our patience? How long shall thy frantic rage baffle the efforts of Justice? To what height meanest thou to carry thy daring insolence? Art thou nothing daunted at the nocturnal host to secure the Palatium? Nothing by the City Guards? ABCDEFGHIJKLMNOPQRSTUVWXYZ ABCDEFGHIJKLMNOPQRSTUVWXYZÆŒ

How far, O Catiline, wilt thou abuse our patience? How long shall thy frantic rage baffle the efforts of Justice? To what height meanest thou to carry thy daring insolence? Art thou nothing daunted at the ABCDEFGHIJKLMNOPQRSTUVWXY £1234567890 ABCDEFGHIJKLMNOPQRSTU MAN MAN

Left: Robert Thorne's display faces of c.1820, based on the distortion of the Modern text face, created a large, powerful type for poster work. The size is the equivalent of present-day 24-point. Fat-face was his most influential face.

Left: A compositor, as the 19th-century typesetter was known, stands at a "frame," setting type from a typecase.

punches and matrices, and proceeded to expand the range of types on offer. His 1798 specimen book contained 45 pages of romans, italics, titlings, shaded letters, flowers, and one font of two-line script. Thorne's fat-face designs were greatly admired. Their reputation spread to the continent, with the result that he received an unprecedented request to cut a fat-face font for the *Imprimerie Royale* in Paris.

Left: A typefoundry's specimen page for Playbill demonstrating the sizes available. This is a 20th-century revival of a 19th-century slab-serif Egyptian in which the serifs have the appearance of being heavier than the letterform itself.

Right: A typical 19th century theater poster, featuring letterforms, slab-serifs, and fat-faces vying for attention.

THE NEW DISPLAY FACES were outsized types that were measured by "lines." A line was the equivalent of one pica (12-points). A common size, six-line for example, would be 72-points.

The first slab-serifs

4

Many display faces were only available as titlings—fonts of capital letters only, that were enlarged on the body, taking up the space normally allocated to the descenders, in order to achieve greater impact.

Just before his early death in 1820, Thorne had been in the process of cutting a slab-serif display type for which he coined the name "Egyptian." The name seemed appropriate since there were parallels drawn between the square black serifs and the relics of ancient Egyptian architecture. It was only a short time after Napoleon's fleet had been defeated in the Battle of the Nile in 1798, and there was a considerable amount of public interest in Egypt due to the Rosetta Stone and other antiquities.

It was, however, Thorne's competitor Vincent Figgins, who created the first slab-serif face in 1815. He named his face "Antique" and produced it in four sizes, all titlings. This was possibly Britain's first truly original contribution to the art of type design. Figgins, a prominent London typefounder, had been apprentice to Joseph Jackson, who himself had been apprentice to William Caslon I. Figgins had managed Jackson's typefoundry during the last years of the latter's life, although he did not manage to take it over after Jackson's death. He was forced to start up on his own, with encouragement from a John Nichols, to whom he later expressed his enormous gratitude. A very capable man, Figgins set up in Holborn, London, soon gaining a reputation as an outstanding, creative typecutter.

The Egyptian slab letterform was a great success, and was soon in use on the continent and in the United States. Over the coming years, the slab-serif was subjected to numerous variations that condensed it into narrow vertical forms or stretched it out to forms that were much wider than they were high.

Vincent Figgins
Antique

Left: Figgins' Egyptian slab-serif design had an extraordinary impact when it was introduced.

Opposite: Figgins' Antique was used extensively alongside Thorne's famed blackletter typeface, as in this poster.

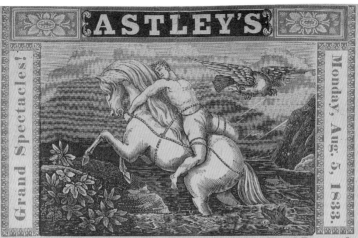

ASTLEY'S

By Desire,—LORD BYRON's interesting and magnificent Drama of

Mazeppa AND THE Wild Horse

. FOR TWELVE NIGHTS ONLY,
WITH NEW SCENERY, DRESSES, AND THE FOLLOWING UNEQUALLED NOVELTY IN THE CIRCLE AND ON THE STAGE:

MR. DUCROW

Will (FOR THE FIRST TIME THESE THREE YEARS) execute on his RAPID COURSER, his popular Scene of the

CARNIVAL OF VENICE;

OR, A MASQUERADE ON HORSEBACK!

AT FULL SPEED;—portraying the following Personages, without quitting the Horse:

PUNCH——PIERO——HARLEQUIN——COLUMBINE——BACCHUS——ADONIS.

Previous to which, (First Time) Mr. DUCROW'S Grand Entree of

24 HIGH-TRAINED STEEDS!

RICHLY CAPARISONED, AND MOUNTED BY DAMES AND CAVALIERS, IN POMPOUS ATTIRE, DELINEATING THE BANQUET CAVALCADE OF

HENRY VIII.

And FRANCIS I., with the HERALDS, KNIGHTS OF OLD, LADIES OF THE COURT, ATTENDANT VASSALS, EQUESTRIAN EVOLUTIONS, and concluding with

A NEW GAVOTTE DANCED BY THE HORSES.

Likewise will be produced, (for the First Time) A NEW COMIC EXTRAVAGANZA, executed by Messrs. A. and J. DUCROW, for the purpose of introducing
THE TRAINED HORSES, called

1st of September, or the Cockney Sportsman!

Mr. JENKINS....Mr. A. DUCROW.   Mr. KILL'EMWRONG....Mr. J. DUCROW.

The SHOOTING PONIES, by the Spanish Horse & Butterfly.

Wonderful Feats of VAULTING, by the Tartar Brothers,

ON A SINGLE HORSE, AT FULL SPEED.

Among the Scenes in the Circle, (for the First Time) Mr. DUCROW'S Pupils and Lilliputian Stud, will appear as the ACTORS OF FAIRY LAND; or, the

TWO IMPORTANT FORMS survived the 19th century's exuberant typographic inventions that went on to be developed in the 20th century: the sans-serif and the resilient slab-serif. The popularity of slab-serifs faded in the latter part of the 19th century, largely due to developments of the typecutter's art, but they experienced a revival in the 1930s.

The new slab-serifs

4

These new slab-serif versions maintained the Egyptian theme. The first to appear was Memphis, from the Stempel Foundry of Frankfurt in 1929. Then came Karnak from Ludlow, and Beton from Bauer in 1931; Cairo from Intertype, and Pharaoh from Deberny & Peignot in 1933; Rock-well from Lanston Monotype in 1934; and Scarab from Stephenson, Blake, & Company in 1937.

The 20th-century slab-serifs were not the extremely assertive extroverts of the previous century. The new types were designed for a modernist aesthetic, and were refined, mono-lined forms with the same kind of geometric purity that was characterisitc of the sans-serifs of the same generation. The serifs are without brackets and have the same thickness as the body strokes, which are modified as the weight increases. These types were specifically designed to be used for text in publicity material,

rather than books, but they are also capable of functioning as display fonts.

The slab-serif, like the sans-serif form, was not only a vigorous survivor of the hot-metal and photosetting periods, but now retains great popularity in the present digital age. The characteristics can be found in the metal typefoundry updates such as Berthold's Beton, Stempel's Memphis, Monotype's Rockwell, and Morris F. Benton's Stymie for ATF, but they can also be found in some new-generation digital fonts. The digitized slab-serif Beton of the Baur Foundry has five weights and no italics; an extremely delicate light, demi-bold, bold, extra bold, and bold condensed. There is an outline shadow version that has not been digitized as yet. Monotype's Rockwell family consisted of light, roman, bold, extra bold, condensed, and bold condensed, each with slanted roman rather than italics. The hot-

ABCDEFGH
abcdefghijk

Slab-serifs have now become more refined than the 19th-century Egyptians. Due to the aesthetics of the 1920s, faces like Rockwell, generally have a single-line thickness with more traditional serif proportions.

metal family included a display titling outline shadow form and a shaded form cross-hatched with fine lines which seem to be a remnant of the 19th century. Stempel's Memphis digitized family provides light, medium, bold, and extra bold. The full hot-metal range included three weights of condensed, an outline version called Open, and Luna, a shadow version. Morris F. Benton's ATF Stymie consists of light, medium, bold, black, and two weights of condensed, medium, and bold. As yet there are no italics or slanted romans.

Rockwell

the quick brown fox jumps over the lazy dog

Memphis

the quick brown fox jumps over the lazy dog

Futura

the quick brown fox jumps over the lazy dog

At first sight Rockwell and Memphis are the same face but Rockwell has a traditional two-storey "a" while Memphis has a single-storey "a," which is favored by the 1927 Futura. The terminal of the vertical stroke of the lowercase "t" also differs, while for Rockwell the dot on the "j" is round, for the Memphis "j" it is square.

ARG
ARG

The differences are more obvious when comparing Rockwell Regular capitals (top), with Memphis Medium capitals.

Above: Pouchée, the French typefounder set up a short-lived typefoundry in London to produce these elaborately decorated display types, produced with the aid of the casting machine invented by Henri Didot.

THE SLAB-SERIF emerged as a new form due to typefounders' search for fresh, eye-catching display letterforms. During the 19th century, as the founders' technical skills improved, more and more elaborate inventions of typographic novelty were created. Typefounders had answered the challenge that the jobbing printers set.

Clarendon

During the early years of the 19th century, the new typeforms were subject to considerable confusion regarding terminology. Foundries invented their own names until later in the century, when many of the more popular forms became part of the jobbing printer's stock of types.

In 1820 Robert Thorne's Fann Street Foundry was taken over by William Thorowgood, who bought it when it was put up for auction. He had no previous connection with typefounding, but threw himself into the business, determined to make a success of his new acquisition. It was said that he had bought the typefoundry with winnings from a state lottery. Thorowgood soon re-established Fann Street on the typographic map, so that by 1822 he had been appointed letterfounder to King George IV. Thorowgood enlarged his collection of punches and matrices, not only by creating his own designs, but also by acquiring the stock from Dr Edmund Fry's typefoundry when he retired. This notable collection included Greek, Hebrew, Russian, and German (blackletter) typefaces.

A MUCH NEEDED ADDITION

In 1845, Thorowgood registered a new type called Clarendon. It is actually Robert Besley who is credited with the origination of this letterform. Besley had worked at the Fann Street Foundry for some ten years and was made a partner in

TWO LINES ENGLISH CLARENDON

Quosque tandem abutere Catilina, patientia nostra? quamdiu nos etiam furor iste tuus eludet? quem ad finem sese effrenata jactabit audacia tua? nihilne te nocturnum præsidium palatii, nihil urbis vigiliæ, nihil timor

£1234567890

METROPOLITAN IMPROVEMENT.

Left: Clarendon was first produced by Thorowgood's Fann Street Foundry in 1845; Robert Besley, a foundry worker later to become a partner, is credited with the design.

12 point
To travel hopefully is a better thing than to arrive, and the true success is to labour.

14 point composition
By appointment to His Royal Highness

14 point display
A Penny Plain and Twopenny Coloured

16 point
An Englishman's house is his castle

18 point
Oliver Twist has asked for more

24 point
Repeal of the Corn Laws

30 point
George Stephenson

36 point
The Lost Chord

42 point
Savoy Operas

12 point
Hazlitt said, as we advance in life, we acquire a keener sense of the value of time.

14 point composition
I dreamt that I dwelt in marble halls

14 point display
The Charge of the Heavy Brigade

16 point
Stockton and Darlington Railway

18 point
The Walrus and the Carpenter

24 point
Victorian Music Halls

30 point
Idylls of the King

36 point
Arts & Crafts

42 point
St. Pancras

1838. This was a face that had its origins in the Egyptian slab-serif, but displayed far more refinement. It showed the thick and thin modeling of a roman, a slight narrowness, and finely bracketed, heavy serifs. It was a bold type cast in text sizes, for Clarendon was designed to emphasize type. The Modern roman was the text face in common use (though the color may have varied from one cutting to another) and was only produced as roman and italics. At this time text typefaces were not cast with a range of different weights, as now. The new typeface was intended to be used with a roman text face in order to emphasize words as required—for example, in dictionaries and similar listings, or to give more impact within the text of advertisements. The bracketing of the serifs was intended to blend the bolder face with the delicate Modern form.

Clarendon proved to be a much needed addition to the printer's range. This was the first type-face design to be registered under England's Designs Copyright Amendment Act. The act prevented the copying of the type for three years. However, because of the popularity of this design, the ban had little effect on the plagiarists; certainly after the three years the specimen books of most foundries carried a version of Clarendon. Among printers, the name "Clarendon" came to be used as a generic term to describe boldness.

Clarendon has maintained an almost unchanged presence in typefounders' specimen books and has not been much extended. In contemporary digitized versions, Hermann Eidenbenz's designs for the Linotype library has three weights, while the Clarendon carried by the Adobe library has a light, medium, bold, and two extra versions; extra bold, and extra bold expanded. Monotype's Clarendon also has three weights, plus a condensed bold. There is no italic form of Clarendon.

THE NEW CENTURY

5

TECHNICAL DEVELOPMENTS

IN THE 19TH CENTURY there was a growing demand for printed material of all kinds—including reading material for entertainment and education, as well as commerce. There were developments in paper manufacturing, reproduction techniques, typefounding, and typesetting.

The Linotype machine, invented by Ottmar Mergenthaler, was demonstrated in New York in 1890. An operator sat at the keyboard and, by depressing the keys, assembled a line of matrices from a magazine above the keyboard. The line of matrices were then cast as one piece of metal, called a "slug," by the injection of molten metal. In 1885 the Monotype machine arrived, which like the Linotype machine, cast type as well as assembling it in lines, but as individual letters rather than slugs.

Stereotyping was a process for making copies of the made-up pages of text and illustrations, known as a "foundry forme," which would be coated with papier-mâché. When dry, it could be used as a flexible mold to make a stereotype of the original forme. This would be used for long print runs when type was likely to wear out; for multiple copies; or for making curved plates for rotary printing presses.

Since the invention of photography there had been numerous attempts to reproduce photographs for printing and in 1888 Frederick Ives of Chicago made this possible with the introduction of the squared screen.

There were innovations in printing presses as well. The first successful machine press was Frederick König's steam-driven stop-cylinder press, constructed in 1812. The pages of type fitted the machine bed, while the paper was wrapped around the cylinder as it passed over the inked type. It was capable of printing 800 copies per hour. König went on to make improvements to his invention. In New York in 1845, Richard Hoe patented a rotary sheet press, on which pages of type were fitted round the cylinder. Three years later, Applegath & Cowper invented the vertical rotary sheet press. Stereotyping was used to make plates that fitted round the cylinders. By 1865, William Bullock had developed the rotary printing press, which used stereotyped plates and printed on a continuous reel, or web, of paper.

Opposite: The Linotype machine solved the need for faster typesetting at the end of the 19th century. The first model appeared in 1890 and combined a keyboard to assemble the matrices and the casting process in one unit. The type was cast as a solid line of letters, called a slug.

Opposite inset: The caster was the second unit that made up the Monotype typesetting system. The two-unit system consisted of a keyboard copy-entry system and a stand-alone caster.

THE COMPLETE MACHINE

61

CONSIDERABLE EFFORT and ingenuity were devoted to the problems of casting and setting type and it was the innovative procedures and devices of Linn Boyd Benton (1844–1932) that contributed most to the improvement of making type. But in the USA and Britain there was still no standard for type measurement.

Adoption of the point system

5

Prior to the development of photosetting and digitization, metal type was processed in two different ways; one created foundry type and the other hot-metal type. Type metal is an alloy, primarily composed of lead with different additions of tin, antimony, and, occasionally, copper. Type alloys had been in existence from the 15th century, and were developed because lead alone was too soft: tin helps the lead melt, while antimony is used to increase hardness and acts to stop the alloy shrinking as it cooled.

Foundry types were the traditional form of metal type that were cast as individual letters for distribution to the typecase for handsetting. The inventions of the 19th century, the single-unit machine Linotype, and the two-unit machine Monotype, were both hot-metal systems. The initial keyboard work selected matrices in order for the type to be cast. After printing, hot-metal type would mostly be returned to the metal pot and melted down to be cast again. Foundry type used a harder alloy, and would be redistributed back to the typecase after printing or stereotyping, ready to be used again—hence the term "printing from moveable type." Today, metal type foundries are very few and far between. If type for handsetting is required, it is most likely to be cast by a Monotype Caster and then distributed to the typecase. Monotype Casters are quite difficult to find, since they are not generally used commercially today.

Linn Boyd Benton became one of the most technically inventive American typefounders. In 1866, he took a job as bookkeeper at the Northwestern Typefoundry, Milwaukee, and soon

Left: The machine punchcutter was a pantographic instrument, invented by Linn Boyd Benton. It became a contributory asset to the manufacturers of Linotype and Monotype typesetting machines.

rose up the ranks. Seven years later, with a partner, he eventually bought the typefoundry.

Benton's first invention in 1882 was a multiple mold for casting typespacing material. He also explored the possibilities of a typesetting machine that had automatic justification. By 1884, his type-foundry was using his most important invention, a pantograph machine for cutting steel punches, which was patented in 1885.

STANDARDIZING THE PICA

France had established a standard measurement for type bodies and related spacing material in 1775, which had spread to other European countries. In America and Britain, however, no agreement about standardization in the industry had been reached, even by the late 19th century. Without pressure from some authority agreement was difficult to achieve, since this would involve many foundries disposing of their existing types and equipment, plunging them into the expensive process of retooling.

A step toward standardization began in America when one of the largest typefoundries, Marder, Luce, & Company, fell victim in 1871 to the Great Chicago Fire, which destroyed their buildings and equipment, molds and type stocks. The company was forced to rebuild and retool, and in the process the directors decided to align their type sizes with those used by MacKellar, Smiths, & Jordan in Philadelphia, the biggest of America's typefoundries.

Nelson Hawks was a junior partner in the unfortunate company, responsible for the office in San Francisco. As a supplier of printers' equipment and materials he was confronted daily with the problems that non-standardization created. He devised a system of type body standardization and was keen to encourage other foundries to participate in it. Eventually his dedication paid

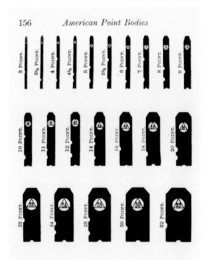

Above: After the Chicago fire of 1871 and years of promotion, Nelson Hawks' standardization of type sizes in the United States was eventually accepted by Britain as well as other English-speaking countries.

off, in spite of resistance from some of his directors, and he was able to convince other foundries of the value of his system. His campaign reached full acceptance in 1886, and was taken up in Britain in 1898. However the MacKellar, Smiths, & Jordan point, which became the universal standard in America, Britain, and other English-speaking countries, is not exactly 72 points to an inch. One point is 1/72.27 of an inch or 0.351mm, which continues to be the standard for metal type. However, Adobe adjusted the point to exactly 1/72 of an inch (0.353 mm) when creating the computer page description program Post-Script in the 1980s, and this is now the standard measurement for digital fonts.

Cheltenham and the Old-style

5

In about 1840, Charles Whittingham, of the Chiswick Press near London, took to using Caslon cast from the original matrices. He printed *Lady Willoughby's Diary* for Longmans book publishers in 1844. While this gained some attention, the revived use of Caslon was considered by some commercial printers and publishers as a retrograde venture. Caslon was not viewed with the same favor as the Modern face. However, Whittingham and a bookseller, William Pickering, went on to use the face for several books, which encouraged others to try it. A decade or so later, Caslon Old-face, which had been forgotten by the Caslon typefoundry, appeared again in the specimen book.

In 1860, the first named "Old-style" type was issued by the typefoundry, Miller & Richard. The publicity assured the reader that the new type design had "removed the distasteful qualities of the Old face while retaining the fundamental characteristics of a pre-Modern face."

Alexander C. Phemister, an employee of the Edinburgh typefoundry, was responsible for the cutting of the Old-style series. He had attempted to adapt the Old-face form to the current aesthetic of the Modern face. The serifs were bracketed and gradual stress was reintroduced, modified to become more vertical, following the modern preference. His typecutting skills gave a uniform

keenness to the forms, eliminating the irregularities of the 18th-century typeface. Shortly after he completed the series in Edinburgh, Phemister settled in America. Working in Boston for the Dickinson typefoundry he cut, among other faces, Franklin Old Style, a similar version to his earlier Old style.

The lighter, more open forms of the Old style gained in popularity over the next few years—aided by some dissatisfaction with the ubiquitous Modern face, and as a result of the more spectacular activities of William Morris and his experiments with the Venetian Old-face of Jenson. There were many copies developed into the early 20th century. There was a tendency for the later Old-styles to emphasize the archaic. They now seem rather mannered. When the machine typesetting companies began their revival of many excellent versions of Old-faces and transitionals, it was with a new respect for the punchcutters of the earlier generations.

Bertram Goodhue was an architect by training, with an interest in typography. In 1894, he designed a typeface for the Merrymount Press of D. B. Updike, based (like Morris' designs) on Jenson's type of 1475. Goodhue had also been involved with the production of a "Chapbook" journal printed by the Cheltenham Press in New York. He was commissioned to design a typeface for the Press's own use. Goodhue set to work with the intention to produce a highly legible design influenced by Old-style characteristics.

Cheltenham Old Style became possibly the most popular American typeface of its time, more for its qualities as a display face than as a text face, and, to a large degree, because of the range of variants available.

Cheltenham has a light, condensed appearance, proportionally short, stubby serifs and an interesting mixture of 20th-century geometric precision and mannered organic forms. This is most noticeable in the vertical stems of the capitals, which contrast with the curved letters of the lowercase "a," "g," "f," "r," and "s." The capital "A" has an overhang at the apex, while the capital "G" has a spur on the lower curve of the bowl which is not quite a serif. It is suitable for publicity texts that need character, since it has a very strong personality on the page.

Above: An example of William Morris' Golden Type in use. Morris chose Nicolas Jenson's Venetian types used in 1476 as a model for his own creation Golden Type.

Above: This 12-point specimen page of 19th-century Old-style is an example of the type that influenced the forms of Bertram Goodhue's later creation, Cheltenham.

AaGg

Above: Bertram Goodhue's Cheltenham Old Style became popular immediately and sparked off a number of similar designs.

Below: Goodhue's design has a distinct character and is rather condensed, with stubby serifs and a small x-height. In this italic cut the lowercase "e" and "p" have open counters, and the "s" has the characteristic terminating teardrop forms rather than serifs.

foremost position

THE AMERICAN PRINTER and printing historian Theodore L. De Vinne was concerned with the state of commercial printing. He had strongly held views on the general standards in commercial printing and what he considered to be the deterioration of the modern letterform but unlike Morris, De Vinne was an experienced and knowledgeable printer with a full understanding of the commercial and practical problems of type design.

De Vinne and New Century

By the close of the 19th century, enormous progress had been made in the development of the printing industry. The demand for books, magazines, newspapers, and other printed matter had hastened technical innovation.

For most of the 19th century, before mechanical typesetting became commonplace, most newspapers and books were printed using a variety of mediocre Modern roman faces. By the early 1800s, British typefounders were producing Modern romans that lacked the full classic elegance of a Bodoni Modern. In their pure simplicity, Bodoni's hairline serifs were not robust enough for the rough handling of the commercial print shop and the power-driven presses; they could only be at their best when given the attention that is possible with the hand press and the smooth surface possible with wove paper, for which they were designed.

There were three British Modern faces that survived the 19th century but were always in the shadow of the internationally respected Bodoni. William Martin, brother Baskerville's apprentice Robert, cut a type for printer William Bulmer in 1790, revived by Morris F. Benton in 1928 as Bulmer. Richard Austin worked for John Bell's British Letter Foundry and cut a transitional type bordering on the Modern that was revived as Monotype Bell in 1932. Later, in 1810, William Miller of Edinburgh commissioned him to cut a Modern, revived in 1909 as Scotch Roman by the American Type Foundry. All three of these owed something to Baskerville, although the vertical contrasting stress of thick and thin strokes expresses the influence of the Modern face. The stress is tapered on curves and serifs carry a suggestion of a bracket, creating a more amiable character that is less austere than Bodoni.

$$Ss\mathit{Kk}$$
$$SsKk$$

Left: De Vinne's type design was not so much a new design as a technical improvement to a Modern face that had not kept up with technological developments. The enlarged image of Century Schoolbook (top) shows that it has something of Clarendon (below) in its character, helping to maintain it as a hard-working, versatile typeface to this day.

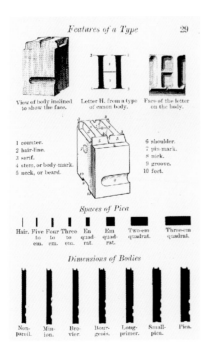

View of body inclined to show the face.

Letter H. from a type of canon body.

Face of the letter on the body.

1 counter.
2 hair-line.
3 serif.
4 stem, or body-mark.
5 neck, or beard.

6 shoulder.
7 pin-mark.
8 nick.
9 groove.
10 feet.

Spaces of Pica

Hair. Five to em. Four to em. Three to em. En quad- rat. Em quad- rat. Two-em quadrat. Three-em quadrat.

Dimensions of Bodies

Non- pareil. Min- ion. Bre- vier. Bour- geois. Long- primer. Small- pica. Pica.

Above: Theodore L. De Vinne (1828–1914) was a frequent writer on the history and practice of printing. He was of the opinion that the delicate

Modern types made popular by Bodoni were unsuitable for the faster printing production methods of mass-market publications.

De Vinne's criticism of these Modern romans was of their poor legibility and presswork. He believed that the uniform vertical stress made identity of individual letters difficult. His proposal for improvement was to increase the thickness of thin strokes and give the serifs more body, not only to improve legibility but also to create a type that was better able to deal with the stresses of the modern machine presses. De Vinne insisted

on keeping the narrow set that was important for maintaining a high number of words per column.

Linn Boyd Benton, as technical director of the American Type Foundry (ATF), was commissioned by De Vinne to cut a type for De Vinne's *Century* magazine. Benton's final design turned out to be a great success, which caused the introduction of a series of variants designed by Boyd's assistant, his son Morris Fuller Benton. Over nearly 30 years Morris Benton developed 18 variants of Century, some of which are now digitized. The most popular digital version of Century is Century Schoolbook, which was released in 1924; other versions are Century Expanded, cut in 1903, and Century Old Style, cut in of 1909.

Below: Century Schoolbook is the most popular of the existing Century family, and is admired for its excellent readability.

abcdefghij
klmnopqr
stuvwxyz
ABCDEFG
HIJKLMN
OPQRSTU
VWXYZ

SANS-SERIF

THE SEARCH FOR typographic originality in the early 19th century led to the introduction of the sans-serif. At the very beginning of the 20th century, the American sans-serif Franklin Gothic was designed. It became one of the most popular Gothics in history, and it retains international celebrity to this day.

Fuller Benton & Franklin Gothic

Morris Fuller Benton began his studies at Cornell University in 1892, the same year that his father's firm, Benton, Waldo, & Company, joined up with 22 other foundries to form the American Type Foundry (ATF). Benton joined ATF as his father's assistant a few months after he graduated. Linn Boyd Benton's energy and inventive genius had made him an important asset to the new organization. Father and son and their families soon moved to New York, closer to head office. By 1900, Benton had become head of ATF's type design department. One of his first projects was the design of a new sans-serif, Franklin Gothic.

Although ATF already had a large number of Gothics in their specimen book as a result of the amalgamation, Benton proceeded to cut the first of the series of Franklin Gothic faces, completed in 1902 and released in 1905. A condensed version was released the same year, the following year saw an extra condensed, oblique fonts came in 1913, and in 1914 a condensed shaded was released. Benton gained a reputation for careful thought and for the research he carried out before commencing a new type design, so it may have been the appearance of revived sans-serifs by the German foundries of Berthold and Bauer

Left: These advertisements in a 1902 motoring magazine are set with typical sans-serifs. Morris Fuller Benton was renowned for his carefully researched approach to type design, and he referred to similar sans-serif fonts found at the American Type Foundry, in redesigning the coherent Franklin Gothic family of weights and styles.

ABCDEFGHIJKLMNOPQRSTUV
abcdefghijklmnopqrstuvwxyz
ABCDEFGHIJKLMNOPQRSTUV

Below: The Franklin Gothic lowercase "g" with its full-looped descender formed into a bowl is typical of the 19th century. The Univers "g" is provided for comparison.

Above: Franklin Gothic has an extensive range of weights and italics, which include a collection of condensed designs.

Right: This Stephenson, Blake, & Company foundry type shows the original forms that are characteristic of the 19th-century sans-serif Grotesque No.9.

that convinced him of the need for a revitalized Gothic. It was the pantographic punchcutting device—which was invented by his father in 1885—that made creating family variants a comparatively simple development.

For the new typeface, the letters were first drawn at about 40mm (1.5") high. Then each letter was produced as a enlarged outline drawing that could be studied for inconsistencies and corrected as necessary. It was also possible at this stage for the pantograph device to be adjusted to draw condensed, expanded, or oblique forms. The improved outline drawing was filled in to make a solid letterform, which was then tested for clarity of form at various sizes, by optical reduction, and again corrected if necessary. A pattern plate was made from the final drawing. This was done by a wax-coated brass plate being fitted to the pantograph machine, and an outline of the drawing being traced at a smaller size

into the wax. A layer of copper was electrically deposited onto the plate in order to create a raised image of the letter. This became the pattern plate, which was used as a template by the punchcutting machine. In the 1960s, ATF develped this punchcutting principal into a machine that engraved directly into matrix blanks, providing a more practical means of making matrices. The machine could be adjusted to engrave matrices of specific point sizes.

Morris F. Benton's Franklin Gothic retained, but refined, features of 19th-century types, such as a slight overall narrowness. There is a modest reduction of line thickness at the junction of stems and bowls, and at the head and foot of circular letters. There is also the retained two-bowl, lowercase "g," which many 20th-century sans-serifs have done away with. Benton's Franklin Gothic has retained its popularity since it has a friendliness matched only by Gill Sans.

AFTER the First World War Germany was unstable and in the face of a collapsing government, many people sought reassurance in strong, dynamic visions of the future. Against this backdrop, it is not surprising that there was considerable enthusiasm for, and hope in, the art movement known as Modernism.

Paul Renner & Futura

There was no new typeface that could express and serve this 20th-century effort to break with the past until well into the 1920s. Futura, issued in 1927 by the Bauer typefoundry, became the favorite and best known of the first geometric sans-serif typefaces that symbolize the aesthetics of early Modernism. Its very name evokes a kind of positive expectation.

Futura was the creation of Paul Renner, a teacher, graphic designer, type designer, and author. Renner was born in the German town of Wernigerode in 1878. He became director of Munich's Graphic Arts College in 1926 and from 1927 was director of the Munich Master Printers' College. During this time he was working on his alphabet design. Renner was an active member of the Deutsche Werkbund. In 1922 he wrote Typography as Art, and in 1932 he wrote Cultural Bolshevism, which later led him into trouble with the National Socialist Party and eventually led to his dismissal from his directorship. In 1933, before his arrest, he was in charge of the design of the German section of the Milan Triennale, and was awarded the Grand Prix.

The modernist aesthetic attached importance to form that derived from function, and ornament and decoration were to be stripped away. Renner took the opportunity in his early studies to explore aspects of letterform that were very different from the conventions for roman forms. At the last moment, when the finished designs were considered for production by the Bauer typefoundry, a number of modifications were recommended to the lower case because the new forms were considered too radical for general commercial use; these were replaced by more conventional forms.

During the early decades of the 20th century the sans-serif emerged as the letterform that best represented the theoretical requirements of avant-garde graphic designers and typographers of the "New Typography."

The sans-serif typeface was a 19th-century invention that emerged from the needs of the industrial age. Its identity was strictly attached to commercial applications, with no connotations of bookishness. In fact, most sans-serifs were display faces, so that when Jan Tschichold was designing his book Die Neue Typographie he had difficulty in finding a text-size sans-serif to use.

The design of a new 20th-century sans-serif was an undertaking that occupied many type designers at this time. Jacob Erbar had claimed the sans-serif as representative of the new age before the war. By 1924, he had produced a sans-serif design named Erbar for the Ludwig & Mayer typefoundry. Rudolf Koch, a highly respected German calligrapher, type designer, and teacher, contributed Kabel, a geometric

Below: The bowls of Futura are not quite circular. Although there is an apparent single-line thickness for stems and bowls, subtle optical corrections at the point of contract between stem and bowl have been made.

abcd

BCGSM
BCGSM

Above: The comparison between the geometric Futura, top, and and humanistic Gill, below, can be appreciated.

sans-serif released by the Klingspor typefoundry in 1927. In England some ten years earlier, Edward Johnston, an expert calligrapher and teacher at the Central School of Arts and Crafts in London, had created a geometric sans-serif intended for use by London Transport.

Futura
the quick brown fox jumps over the lazy dog

Helvetica
the quick brown fox jumps over the lazy dog

Univers
the quick brown fox jumps over the lazy dog

Gill Sans
the quick brown fox jumps over the lazy dog

Above: Renner's poster design for the college uses the letterforms that he had developed for his successful geometric sans-serif, Futura.

Left: A comparison of four 20th-century sans-serifs makes it easier to appreciate their individual characters.

ALTHOUGH THE EARLY part of the 20th century was notable for the arrival of new sans serif faces in 1930 there was an exception, Times New Roman, a typeface created for the *Times* newspaper, that became associated with authority and the British Empire.

Stanley Morison & Times

While the actual creator of the design is to this day a source of controversy, it is undisputed that Morison was responsible for the introduction of this type, and it fitted the purpose beautifully.

In the 1930s, Stanley Morison was at the height of his power and influence as an authority on letterforms and type history. He was an established commentator on the art of printing and wrote extensively on the history of early printing. He has been described as possibly the most distinguished British scholar and typographer of the 20th century.

Morison started his working life as a clerk. In 1913, his first printing job was at the office of

Imprint, a journal that campaigned for an awareness of good printing and design. In 1923 he co-founded *The Fleuron*, a journal of typography which won international acclaim with its articles on typographic history and theory. He also took on the post of typographic adviser to Cambridge University Press and the Monotype Corporation.

Below: Morison's redesign not only consisted of producing a text typeface. He wrote a detailed analysis of what were the existing faults and an explanation of what was needed. This consisted of several versions of the new type to fulfil particular functions, such as the small advertisements that still appeared on the front page.

"THE TIMES" IN NEW TYPE

HOW THE CHANGE WAS MADE

The change of type completed with this morning's issue of *The Times* has involved one of the biggest undertakings ever accomplished in a newspaper office. More than two years have been devoted to designing and cutting the type charac-

"THE TIMES"

LAST DAY OF THE OLD TYPE

MONDAY'S CHANGES

The Times appears to-day for the last time in the type to which the present generation has grown accustomed.

On Monday the changes already an-

In 1929, Morison contributed to a special *Times* newspaper supplement on printing. His article, "Newspaper Types: A Study of The Times," was highly critical of the quality of the newspaper's printing and old-fashioned typography. He produced a lengthy report, which put his case for the improvements to the paper's typefaces; making proposals in the light of type history and the qualities of various type designs, and introducing ideas from the latest research on legibility.

Morison believed that the newspaper had to improve its printing quality so that it reached the standard normal for books. Due to his interest in historic typefaces and his role of supervising the revival and commissioning of typefaces for the Monotype Corporation, Morison had in mind a modified version of the typeface Plantin, improved with sharper serifs to give the type better definition for stereotyping casting. Since he himself was no draftsman, to realize his ideas Morison made use of the drawing skills of Victor Lardent, a lettering artist employed in the advertising department of *The Times*.

The task wasn't straightforward. After many drawings and test castings, the revised style of *The Times* was launched on 3 October 1932. The previous typeface used by the newspaper had been known as Times Old Roman, so its replacement was named Times New Roman.

Times New Roman

the quick brown fox jumps over the lazy dog

Garamond

the quick brown fox jumps over the lazy dog

Baskerville

the quick brown fox jumps over the lazy dog

Bodoni

the quick brown fox jumps over the lazy dog

Left: As a serif typeface Times New Roman has a crisp, clean neutrality that has recommended it to the general printing industry. It has a large x-height and is rather narrow, which makes it very economic on space; this is an important quality for a newspaper type. Its sturdy letterforms were designed to withstand the rigors of letterpress newspaper presses.

TT
RR

Above: The economic design of Times New Roman, shown in black are compared with the same letters of John Baskerville's roman, shown gray.

LETTER CARVER, wood engraver, and sculptor Eric Gill was born in Brighton, England in 1882. He was apprenticed to the architect of the Ecclesiastical Commission of London. Here he developed an interest in carving lettering and attended evening classes run by the brilliant calligrapher, Edward Johnston.

Eric Gill & his Sans-Serif

On leaving the architect's office in 1903, Gill set up on his own as a craftsman in a workshop in Hammersmith, West London. There he took on commissions of lettering and wood engraving for (among others) W. H. Smith and the publishers Insel, based in Leipzig, Germany.

Gill moved to the Sussex village of Ditchling in 1906. Here he was able to extend his skills to include carving sculpture. The artistic community of Ditchling developed with the arrival of Edward Johnston and Douglas Pegler, who brought a small handpress workshop which became known as the St Dominic Press.

Seven years older, Stanley Morison was 33 when he became the typographical advisor to the Monotype Corporation in 1923. Morison was not a supporter of the Modern design movement, favoring rather the classical book design of the pre-19th-century master printers. Morison held the responsibility for providing a program of re-cutting historic typefaces, and to commission new contemporary typefaces to extend the range of Monotype composition faces. Late in 1925, Morison invited Gill to help him in this. Gill was a good choice, because although he had no previous experience of the technical requirements that were involved, he had been an enthusiastic creator of letterforms since childhood.

The first typeface that Gill designed for Morison, without either of them having much

abcdefghijklmnopqrstuv
wxyz & ABCDEFGHIJKL
MNOPQRSTUVWXYZ
1234567890

Above: Eric Gill's best-known humanist sans-serif is Gill Sans. The first types appeared in 1928.

A a G g
A a G g

Compared with Futura, Gill Sans shown black, is less mechanical; its forms reminiscent of classical roman proportions.

By Eric Gill

SCULPTURE
AND
THE LIVING
MODEL

Sheed & Ward

Left: Gill with his son-in-law and partner René Hague, designed and printed this book in 1929.

Right: A page from a 1930 edition of The Fleuron Society's journal set in inscriptional style, using 14-point Gill Titling.

MAY 31
COLLECT FOR
THE FEAST OF S. ANGELA MERICI

DEUS, QUI NOVUM PER BEATAM ANGELAM SACRARUM VIRGINUM COLLEGIUM IN ECCLESIA TUA FLORESCERE VOLUISTI: DA NOBIS, EIUS INTERCESSIONE, ANGELICIS MORIBUS VIVERE; UT, TERRENIS OMNIBUS ABDICATIS, GAUDIIS PERFRUI MEREAMUR AETERNIS · PER DOMINUM NOSTRUM IESUM CHRISTUM FILIUM TUUM QUI TECUM VIVIT ET REGNAT IN UNITATE SPIRITUS SANCTI DEUS PER OMNIA SAECULA SAECULORUM

ABCDEFGHIJJKLMN
OPQQRRSTUV
WXYZ

1.2,3:4·5-6!7?8§9*¶()[ ]

Gill's resulting sans-serifs were firmly modelled on classic roman proportions. Gill was able to introduce refinements, which, with the help of the Monotype drawing office, have established Gill Sans as a much-loved classic among sans-serifs. The first of the series to be published in 1928 was a titling available in five sizes (14-point, 18-point, 24-point, 30-point, and 36-point); a lowercase version did not appear until 1933. Since then there have been additional variants, many of them not from Gill's hand.

In contrast to the geometric sans-serifs of the same decade, Gill Sans has a friendly warmth and is classified as a humanist sans-serif. The series was originally produced as hot-metal letterpress type, so when it was digitized it is most likely that the original Monotype office drawings were used.

idea of how to proceed, was called Perpetua. The letterforms are uniquely Gill's, reflecting his experience of lettercutting in stone. Perpetua is a classically proportioned roman with smoothly bracketed, sharply tapering serifs.

It was during this time that the idea for Gill's famous sans-serif emerged. While working on Perpetua, in 1926, Gill was asked to paint a shop sign for a Bristol bookseller, Douglas Cleverdon. It was this lettering that led Morison to suggest that Gill create a sans-serif to compete with the continental geometric sans-serifs that were beginning to become popular. The letterform Gill had created for the shop was only a capital alphabet and he embarked on the design aware of the greater difficulties of constructing an even monoline lowercase alphabet, which involved many curves and junctions.

HELVETICA HAS FOUND enduring popularity from the 1960s onward. Arial, distributed by Microsoft, is an unauthorized, Helvetica clone, and can be distinguished from Helvetica by examining the uppercase "R." It's also a default typeface for the Mac OS.

Miedinger & Helvetica

Although the Swiss Modernists of the 1940s were supporters of sans-serif as a basic typeface for modern graphic design, they did not make use of Renner's Futura, the sans-serif of the 1920s. They did not care for the cool geometry of its letterforms and preferred the late-19th-century Grotesques. The sans-serif letterforms introduced originally as display type had at first been described as "Grotesques" because, while they were acknowledged to be effective graphically, they did not meet the prevailing standards of elegance. In the 1940s and 1950s, however, prevailing opinion believed the monoline forms to be clear, open, and legible, without historical or social connotations.

Many of the 19th-century Grotesques (for example, the Stephenson, Blake, & Company's Grotesque No.8 and No.9) were unsuitable for revival, being too bold, too condensed, or simply too idiosyncratic. One of the first to be brought back was Akzidenz-Grotesk, the Berthold sans-serif of 1898. This was a well-proportioned,

clearly-formed sans-serif with no outstanding idiosyncrasies.

Those who objected to the total use of sans-serif considered the Grotesques to be lacking unsubtlety and legibility compared with the serifed letterform. While sans-serifs might be used in advertising display, they were totally unsuitable for lengthy texts. Serifs, critics argued, improved legibility by forming visual links between letters, enabling them to fit together better as words.

As the economic situation improved and typefoundries returned to full production in the 1950s, a process of upgrading began to take place. Along with other foundries, the Haas typefoundry in Münchenstein, Switzerland, searched for suitable typefaces for modernization. In the mid-1950s the directors Edouard and Alfred Hoffmann briefed their in-house designer Max

First cast as foundry type for hand-setting, New Haas Grotesque was available in a limited number of body sizes. Later in the 1960s as Helvetica, it became available for machine setting.

ABCDEFGHIJKLMNOPQRSTUVWXYZ&
abcdefghijklmnopqrstuvwxyz.,;:!?-'()
£1234567890

Miedinger with their plan to produce a new sans-serif to meet the growing demand and competition for typefaces.

Miedinger's choice as a model for his design was an 1880 type, Schelter Grotesk. The sans-serif that Miedinger produced in 1956 was released as Neue Haas Grotesk. The first version consisted of three weights; medium, semibold, and bold, with no italics. It was cast in 13 sizes, from six to 48-point, as foundry type for handsetting. At the time this was still a common method of typesetting, especially for display work. When the Haas parent company, the D Stempel AG typefoundry in Frankfurt, released Neue Haas Grotesk in West Germany in 1961, they renamed it Helvetica, the Latin word for Swiss. This made reference to Swiss International Style and was considered a more suitable name for international purposes. Helvetica was not, actually, that popular with the Swiss, possibly due to the competition from Akzidenz Grotesk, which was well-entrenched. However, in other European countries Helvetica became popular with those sympathetic to Swiss graphic design philosophy. In 1983 Helvetica was digitized by the Linotype Design Studio and updated with a comprehensive range of family variants, released as Neue Helvetica.

The blandness of Miedinger's New Haas Grotesque design may have held the secret of its success. It was commissioned by Edouard Hoffman, who also commissioned Herman Eidenbenz in the design of Clarendon.

Dans les nombreux commentaires et analyses de la bonne affiche, qui s'occupent de la qualité et du niveau de l'efficacité, nous regrettons de **ne trouver rien** qui relève spécifiquement des capacités solides, ni aucune étude des facteurs qui ont assuré à l'affiche suisse sa place à part. Les commentateurs ont admis jusqu'à présent le niveau moyen élevé de ce secteur graphique particulier comme allant de soi, sans se rendre

28

Hôtel-Pension Métropole
Abonnement de parcours
MAGASINS DU LOUVRE
EXPOSITION MONDIALE

36

Chemische Färberei
Amtliches Kursbuch
WOCHEN-ZEITUNG
HANDELSKAMMER

48

Nationalkassen
Quartalberichte
REICHENSTEIN

Im Gegensatz zur dokumentarischen Aufnahme, wie sie beispielsweise mit Vorzug in der Industrie-Werbung verwendet wird, ist die **Photographie** mit Bewegung oder bei mehrschichtiger Gruppierung ein Mittel, um Geheimnis oder Dynamik ins Bild zu bringen. Wir wollen hier nicht erforschen, inwieweit diese Art der Photographie berechtigt ist und ob auch die gezeigten Beispiele bedachtvoll auf ihren Verwendungszweck bezogen sind. Wichtig erschien uns, diese Serie sehr gut gelungener Photos zu reproduzieren. Sie verraten einen wachen Sinn für die Möglichkeit

HELVETICA IS CLASSIFIED as a Neo-grotesque sans-serif, as it is modeled on 19th-century Grotesques. Others included in this classification are Akzidenz Grotesk, Venus, Haas Unica, Grotesque No. 1, Berthold Standard Grotesk, and Folio.

Helvetica: the typeface

Helvetica has proved to be one of the most popular sans-serifs of all time. This must be due in some degree to the inclusion of the font in many computer systems. Its great success has made it subject to many imitations, which include Arial, Helious, Swiss, Helvetia, Nimbus, and Heldustry.

The refurbished 19th-century Grotesques gained favor because they presented a simple, unadorned, neutral character that expressed, better than any other designs, the requirements of the 20th-century Modernist aesthetic. Modernist typographers, like their traditionalist counterparts, considered it important that text types be as neutral as possible, so that the type exerts a minimal influence on the mood of the reader. Both Akzidenz-Grotesk and Helvetica were designed with this in mind.

Helvetica is a typeface associated originally with the Swiss International Style; now, however, like Times New Roman, it has become popular

hhhhh**hhh**
hhhhhhhh
hhhhh**hhh**
hhhhhhhh
hhhhh**hhh**
hhhhhhh

Right: The promotional brochure for Helvetica is an exemplar of the Swiss Style. Helvetica was marketed very successfully and it quickly became fashionable on its release in 1961.

Helvetica has become possibly the most used sans-serif ever. Neue Helvetica consists of a large range of weights, from Ultra Light to Black, in roman, condensed, and expanded forms.

Satzanwendungen und Druckbeispiele

and ubiquitous. It is used in many different ways for many different purposes, proving its value as a font with clear, no-nonsense legibility, making its point without rhetoric. Helvetica's core weights make it a very legible, and it has a large x-height, fairly short ascenders and descenders, and close letter fit. The letterforms—both capitals and lowercase—are generously shaped; the "O" is almost, but not quite, a full circle. Helvetica is hard to differentiate from Akzidenz Grotesk, the differences lying in the details. Helvetica has a larger x-height; the terminals of curved letters "C," "G," "S," "a," "c," "e," and "s" are horizontal, when in Akzidenz they are closer to 45 degrees. This is more noticeable in heavier weights.

The original D Stempel AG Helvetica, the preferred range of 1961, is now digitized, and contains a range of four weights with obliques from light to black in standard set width. Helvetica Condensed has four weights with obliques from light to black, and there are two weights of Helvetica Narrow and one weight of Helvetica Compressed, Extra Compressed, and Ultra Compressed. There is one weight of Inserat Roman and there are three fonts of Helvetica Rounded (the font is made less austere by the stems being rounded off at the terminals). There are also two textbook weights and a range of numerical fractions—a total of 19 variations in the family. The 1983 digitized range of Neue Helvetica contains eight weights and obliques from ultra light to bold outline in standard set width. Neue Helvetica Condensed has 10 weights and obliques from ultra light to extra black oblique. Neue Helvetica Extended has eight weights and obliques from ultra light extended to black extended oblique—a total of 26 variations in the family. Digital innovation has meant font variants are far more simple to produce than before, and Helvetica shows how the concept of the font family maybe extended to the limits to offer a truly comprehensive palette.

Helvetica

the quick brown fox jumps over the lazy dog

Univers

the quick brown fox jumps over the lazy dog

Futura

the quick brown fox jumps over the lazy dog

Left: It is interesting to compare three of the most prominent sans serif faces of the 20th century. Futura appears very idiosyncratic compared with the other two. Its lower case "j" has no finial and the "u" has no stem.

Ga

Ga

Compare the letterforms "G" and "a" of Helvetica (Grotesque) and Franklin (Gothic).

PHOTOSETTING

6

IN 1954, the Deberny & Peignot typefoundry in Paris was preparing a typeface collection for the new Lumitype/Photon photosetting machine. A sans-serif was required and Futura was a strong possibility, until Charles Peignot's young design director Adrian Frutiger asked for the opportunity to submit a design of his own. Univers was the resulting typeface.

Frutiger had been given ten days to prepare his proposal and he drew 16 versions of his sans-serif using the five letters that formed the word "monde." Peignot was delighted with Frutiger's designs and names were discussed: "Le Monde" was rejected as being too French. Eventually at Peignot's insistence it was called "Univers."

Frutiger had been trained in a sans-serif environment dominated by Akzidenz Grotesk. While studying under Walter Käch he had prepared some drawings for a sans-serif, so for his proposal he returned to his student work. His new sans-serif for the Lumitype/Photon photosetting system was a fresh look at the form; the new technology influencing a move away from the 19th-century monoline. The new sans-serif introduced a variation of line thickness, so that there is a slight difference between vertical and horizontal strokes, creating a more refined form than the metal letterpress monoline Grotesques.

As a typeface designed for photosetting, the new type was intended to fulfil the role of a sans-serif for extended lengths of text as well as display. Its first release in 1957 consisted of 21 variants within a carefully rationalized system conceived from the first set of drawings. Frutiger had given much thought to the issue of type families, which in many cases were created by an ad hoc process of adding further weights to a face as it acquired acceptance.

Frutiger introduced a numbering system related to a grid to identify the family relationships. The regular weight was 55, what would normally be bold was 65, extra bold was 75, and light was 45. Regular weight italic was 56, 66 was bold italic, 76 was extra bold italic, and 46 was light italic. The grid also explained the relationships within the family: to the right were increasingly condensed variants, to the left increasingly extended variants.

Opposite: The rationalizing of the family was a milestone in type design—a development combined with the refinement of the sans-serif letterform. Although Univers met with resistance in Switzerland from Akzidenz Grotesk and Neue Haas Grotesk, it was generally hailed as an innovation.

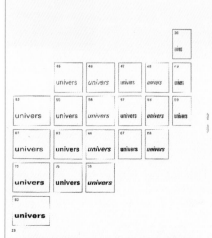

39				
				univers
45	46	47	48	49
	univers	univers	*univers*	*univers*	univers
53	55	56	57	58	59
univers	univers	*univers*	univers	*univers*	univers
63	65	66	67	68
univers	univers	*univers*	univers	*univers*
73	75	76
univers	univers	*univers*
83
univers

23

végétal précieux **compact** *léger* **fort** faible *rapide* **lourd** stable

24

25

So bin ich unversehens ein Landschaftsmaler geworden. Es ist entsetzlich. Wenn man in eine Sammlung neuerer Bilder gerät, welch eine Menge von Landschaften gibt es da; wenn man in die Gemäldeausstellung geht, welch eine noch größere Menge von Bildern trifft man da an. Ich rede hier gar nicht

Porbus s'inclina respectueusement, et il laissa entrer le jeune homme en le croyant amené par le vieillard, s'inquiéta d'autant moins de lui que le néophyte demeura sous le charme que doivent éprouver les peintres-nés à l'aspect du premier atelier qu'ils voient et où se révèlent quelques-uns des matériaux

I have just come down from the hill fronting my home in mid-Cardiganshire. It is like half a hundred hills in this part of Wales, rounding out of a bramble-filled dingle on the southern side, a dingle blue-black with juiced fruit in autumn, with a sun-shot fringe of scrub oak and alder, and a noble ash-tree

23 The 21 different founts of Univers. A decimal system of classification indicates variations of weight and width; 40 for light, 50 for medium, 60 for bold, and so on; 3 denotes expanded, 7 condensed, 9 extra condensed. Uneven numbers are used for italics, even numbers for italic.

24 Contrasts between thick and thin strokes vary with different weights and widths, but height and depth remain constant, and letter forms preserve a family likeness. Variants can therefore be mixed.

25 The construction of letters is consistent in all the different letters of this alphabet. A similarity of appearance is therefore preserved, even with settings in different languages, with differing letter frequencies.

26 The small difference in height between capitals and lower case ensures a well-balanced composition.

27 Joining strokes are slightly thickened. Spottiness is avoided by giving slightly conical shapes to all letters which have joining strokes.

28/29 Optical, not mathematical, rules govern the weight and height of letters.

30 How different weights and widths are balanced.

26

27

28

29

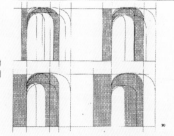

30

UNIVERS'S GREAT QUALITY is its modesty. What Adrian Frutiger's design may lack as an assertive display face, it makes up for in its quietly efficient range of weights, enabling it to function as a text face as well as for display.

Frutiger & Univers

Despite its divergence from Helvetica and Akzidenz-Grotesk, Univers is essentially a Neo-grotesque, but with a humanist touch. The earliest version of Univers was designed for use on the Lumitype/Photon photosetting machine, which was a second-generation photosetter. However, its popularity increased when, in 1961, Monotype released it for Monophoto and hot-metal machines. The sizes for hot metal were actually continental Didot point sizes cast on larger Anglo-American point bodies, as the Didot point was larger than the Anglo-American point. This was possibly an economy, since the demise of the hot-metal Monotype system had already been signaled by the first Monophoto Filmsetter's introduction in 1957.

A comparison with Helvetica and Akzidenz shows Univers to be narrower, more noticeably in the capitals. The circular characters are more oval, with a slight squareness to the curves,

abcdefghijklmnop
qrstuvwxyz
ABCDEFGHIJKLMN
OPQRSTUVWXYZ
abcdefghijklmnop
qrstuvwxyz

Left: As a sans-serif, Univers is classified as a Neo-grotesque, implying its form is influenced, if only a little, by the 19th century Grotesques.

Below: The Univers italic (shown black) is much squarer and more condensed than Helvetica italic (gray).

e *e*
e e

suggesting a less mechanical form. However, the letterfit is more generous, so that size for size, even though the x-height is smaller, Univers will take up more space than Helvetica. The range of variants follows carefully balanced increases in weight that do not match those of Helvetica and Akzidenz.

The slight slimming of horizontal curves, more associated with serif forms, is intended to overcome the optical illusion that makes horizontal strokes appear thicker than vertical ones. In addition to the overall general character of Univers, there are some individual letters which identify it; the "C" has a wide mouth, and "G" is without a spur at the foot (this is characteristic of Frutiger's sans-serifs although more common in serif fonts). The arms of "K" join each other at a single point on the vertical stem, and "Q" has a tail that lies along the baseline. Among the lowercase characteristics, the "a" has no spur on the vertical stem, the ascender of "t" is cut diagonally, and

"g" has a tail rather than a bowl—a common characteristic of this generation of sans-serifs.

During the late 1990s, in addition to their existing range of Univers, Linotype took on the task of totally updating the 40-year-old design. This involved a return to the original drawings of the 1950s to check up on the anomalies that might have arisen during the years Univers had been in circulation. Linotype has updated the design by carrying out refinements to the letterforms and the character weight relationships, and the range of weights and widths has been increased. Italics have become obliques, and the angle of slant has also been increased. The original two-digit numbering system has been revised and a three-digit system replaces it. In the new system, the first digit denotes the weight, the second denotes the width, and the third digit denotes whether it is roman or italic.

This typographic diagram explains in purely visual terms the relation and the numbering system applied to the 21 variants of Univers.

Above: Both these typefaces appeared in the 1950s. The subtle variation of line thickness when set against Helvetica (shown black) reveals Univers (gray) to be more organic in detail.

BACK TO THE FUTURE

ZAPF & OPTIMA
ZAPF & PALATINO

HERMANN ZAPF is another great typographer of the 20th century. Like Frutiger, he has been confronted by the changing technologies of 20th-century type design. Zapf is exactly ten years older than Frutiger, and was born into a time of revolution.

Zapf & Palatino

In 1935, Zapf went to an exhibition of the work of the famous Nuremberg calligrapher and type designer Rudolf Koch. He was immediately entranced and fascinated by the lettering and type designs of the artist-craftsman. Zapf then spent many hours teaching himself calligraphy with a broad pen. When his employer discovered his calligraphic abilities, he was given lettering to retouch.

Through acquaintance with the printing historian Gustav Mori, Zapf came into contact with the D Stempel AG typefoundry and Linotype GmbH in Frankfurt. By 1938, he designed his first typeface, cut by August Rosenberger. It was a fraktur (a kind of blackletter) design called Gilgenart.

The first of Zapf's outstanding typefaces was Palatino, designed by Zapf and cut by August Rosenberger, produced after much careful study with Rosenberger. Zapf's knowledge and love of calligraphy were manifest in this mid-20th century typeface. Palatino is a tribute to the work of Giovanbattista Palatino, the writing master of Rome and author of a popular writing manual in 1540.

After two years of tests, Palatino was released in 1950. The name expresses Zapf's gratitude to the Renaissance, but the making of the typeface made full use of the printing technology of the 20th century.

Even from a cursory look at Palatino it is immediately clear that the thick and thin stems suggest the kind of strokes made by the broad pen. It is a chunky, sturdy type with a large x-height, which has not reduced the length of the ascenders or descenders. In fact, the ascenders are taller than the capitals; this is the same relation normally found in late Renaissance faces and their neohumanist descendents. A large x-height makes larger open counters possible and improves legibility. In the early days after the war this was an important consideration, because the paper available for printing was of poor quality. The early version of the design had a heavier stroke thickness compared with most roman typefaces, which was considered better for adapting to the requirements of the lithographic and gravure processes in use at the time. There is considerable subtlety of form and dramatic features in the letters: not only in the move from thick to thin of the strokes, but also in the vertical stems, which swell as they meet the serifs at the head and foot. The circular letters have a fullness that derives from the "O" being wider than it is high, and the tail of the "Q" is definitely a flourish of the pen below the baseline. The capital "X" has a curved one-sided serif on the thick stroke, and on the thin stroke an inner serif is non-existent. In the case of the capital "Y," the left arm emulates the "X," while the thin right arm swells but is without a serif. "S" has a tight changing curve that suggests contained energy. The italic alphabet has a classic calligraphic form expressed by the repeated shape of the bowls of "a," "b," "o," "p," and "q."

In 1954, as the quality of paper improved, Zapf produced an additional lighter version of Palatino, which was to overcome the perception that the existing Palatino weights were too heavy for book work. At first called Palatino Light Book, the font was later released as Aldus. The one weight with italic has been digitized, and it has now become a face in its own right with additional weights, more recently being redesigned and available as Aldus Nova.

Right: Zapf's achievements in type design have made him a major figure of postwar typography. His typefaces reflect his love of calligraphy, combined with an appetite for the challenge of new typographic technology. An annotated version is shown of Zapf's Palatino.

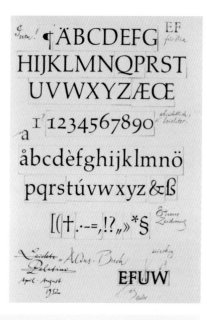

abcdefghijklmnop
qrstuvwxyz
ABCDEFGHIJKLMN
OPQRSTUVWXYZ
abcdefghijklmnop
qrstuvwxyz

Left: Palatino reflects Zapf's love of calligraphy, particularly in the italic.

RX
RX

The heavier line weight and subtle flourishes of Palatino (shown black) can be seen when compared with Adobe Caslon (gray).

IT IS INTERESTING to compare Zapf's work with that of the other great 20th-century type designer Adrian Frutiger, to see just how their different aesthetics and motivating philosophies emerged in the forms they gave their letters. Frutiger's designs are informed by a Modernist geometric aesthetic. Zapf's influences reach back to the Renaissance and earlier, to times when handwriting had cultural importance.

Zapf & Optima

Zapf's sans-serif type design, Optima, is a case in point, a remarkably original typeface created at a time when many foundries were releasing their updated 19th-century Grotesques. The letterforms were developed from impromptu sketches Zapf made of inscriptions, which he observed at the fourth-century Arch of Constantine in Rome and inlaid on the floor of the Santa Croce, Florence, while on a visit to Italy in 1950. The pronounced stress of thick and thin strokes, the swelling of the stems at their terminals, and the thinning of

curves have created a sans-serif that has achieved a balance between the drawn sans-serif forms of the machine age and the pen-written serif forms of the Renaissance. The result is a delicate sans-serif with a strong desire to be a serif type.

The first Optima design was intended to be available only in display sizes. Zapf completed the designs in 1952 after the usual legibility tests. At the same time he was deeply engaged with the design of another of his important typefaces, Melior, which was designed for the specific needs

abcdefghijklmnop
qrstuvwxyz
ABCDEFGHIJKLMN
OPQRSTUVWXYZ
abcdefghijklmnop
qrstuvwxyz

Left: The variation of line thickness betrays the inscriptional character of Optima's original influence. This is particularly evident in the Optima "G" and "M" (shown black) as compared with those of Univers (gray).

GM
GM

of high-speed newspaper printing. However, in 1954 Zapf reconsidered his plans for Optima. This was a result of a suggestion from Monroe Wheeler of the Museum of Modern Art in New York that the design should be available for text setting as well.

Optima was not released by D Stempel AG until 1958, initially as metal foundry type. Shortly afterward it was converted for hot-metal slug setting by Linotype GmbH. It became one of Zapf's most successful designs.

Optima is best suited to situations in which Grotesques are too utilitarian, and serif forms too bookish. The current digitized range of Optima contains 12 variants: roman, medium, demibold, bold, black, and extra black, each including a companion "italic." These so-called "italic" fonts are actually slanted roman (or obliques). The heavier weights maintain the family resemblance but not the elegance. This arises from the relationship of the thick and thin stresses: as the weight is increased the proportions change.

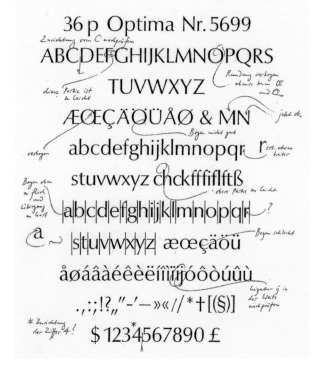

Above: Optima lowercase (shown black) is compared above with Frutiger's Univers (gray), which was released a year before Optima. The subtle changes of line thickness of Optima (the darker type) hint at serifs.

Right: The design of a typeface goes through many stages of modification before it is finally released for use. Zapf's annotations here are mostly concerned with the sidebearings and quality of letter fit.

DIGITAL TYPE

A NEW WAVE OF TYPOGRAPHIC DESIGN

THE PERSONAL COMPUTER
DIGITAL TYPE FORMATS
DIGITAL TYPE FOUNDRIES

AFTER SOME 40 YEARS of typography and graphic design based on the 1920s' theorists and consolidated by the Swiss School, the International Style was ready for reassessment. Modernism had always had its critics, but this was a reassessment that was more sustained.

A new wave of typographic design

There were basically two modes of repudiation: the instinctive or emotional, on the part of designers who felt inhibited by the Modernist rationale; and the theoretical, mostly on the part of educators who felt the need to advance change in the light of more recent developments in communications, and so searched for a new rationale for design in the latter part of the 20th century.

In Switzerland, the home of the International Style, the designs that Siegfried Odermatt and Rosemarie Tissi produced displayed a mischievous disregard for the clarity and order that were the norm in Swiss design. They introduced staggered columns of text, angled ragged columns, and used panels of color to divide up the format or highlight the shape of columns of type. Bold letterforms overlapped each other in colorful heaps, yet the message was never obscured.

In Britain, a younger graphic designer, Neville Brody, started work in the record industry in the late 1970s, just as punk rock began to cause outrage in the tabloid newspapers. A spirit of rebellion was already present in the work that Brody had produced as a student in the design department of the London College of Printing.

Brody became the art director of *The Face* magazine and proceeded, with the editor Nick Logan, to create one of the most exciting youth

Left: Siegfried Odermatt and his partner Rosemarie Tissi began producing designs that rejected Swiss typographic formalism. The grid was neglected and patches of text where emphasized by panels of color, so that the surface of the design appeared to be layered. The example was for the Swiss printing house Buchdruck-Offsetdruck Anton Schob.

Left: Not since the 1960s had a youth magazine's visual style created as much interest as Brody's design for The Face did. The mixing of typefaces within words at this time was generally achieved by the technique of cut-and-paste—a term that has been retained for the desktop computer.

magazines of the period. There was a strong challenge from Terry Jones's small-format but radical youth magazine *I-D*, which also rejected current concepts of "good taste" typography, and reported on authentic street fashions. Neville Brody, through the work he created for the pop music industry and youth magazines, became possibly the first graphic designer to be raised to the status of a celebrity, stimulating interest in graphic design among the next generation. Graphic design was becoming sexy.

Wolfgang Weingart suggested that Swiss design was value-free; that is, it simply presented a message free from additional visual characteristics that heightened persuasiveness.

Weingart consolidated his approach in his introduction of an advanced program that was to be based on the examination of fundamental concepts in typography, such as the predominance of the right angle and the grid, and an intuitive response to the organization of space.

Among Weingart's students at this time were the Americans Dan Friedman and April Greiman.

Right: Brody's 1981 sleeve design for the post-punk band 23 Skidoo rejected the conventional typographic refinement of most logotypes.

In his book *Radical Modernism*—his term for the break away from the International Style—Friedman discussed the issues surrounding the New Wave. He expressed the view that the well-structured readability which Swiss typography had achieved created a predictability that failed to stimulate the reader's interest. In his opinion, unpredictability was required to stimulate a more positive response in the reader.

April Greiman emphasized a playful quality that explored illusions of three-dimensional space, visual textures created with enlarged half-tones and video screens, rules, and brush marks. She also made use of early low-resolution computer-generated letterforms.

IN 1985 THERE BEGAN a revolution in the way typefaces are created and used. Three companies, Apple, Adobe, and Aldus combined forces to create what came to be known as desktop publishing. And an unfamiliar term was added to our vocabulary, the font, a digital file containing all the information needed to reproduce a typeface.

The personal computer

8

In the days when type was set by hand, the fount, as it was originally known, was a complete set of letters of a typeface in one particular size and style—lower case, caps, punctuation mark, and symbols. Over time the "u" disappeared and printers and typesetters referred to it as a font.

The revolution had begun 20 years earlier with the introduction of photosetting which combined with offset lithography were very important aids to greater freedom and refinement in typographic design. The bromide print outputs from phototypesetting machines, rather than an inked proof, made the handling of text and display type easier for cut-and-paste page make-up. The manipulation of type and images was no longer limited by the heavy and to some degree clumsy strictures of letterpress. The horizontal and vertical that were so important to the physics of metal typesetting were no longer important. Type was generated photochemically, therefore type no longer had a body, only a face. This allowed for refinements such as the adjustment of space between letters (tracking), so that it could be increased or reduced from the normal spacing.

Left: The Apple Macintosh 128K (The "Mac") with its unique Graphical User Interface (GUI) was introduced in 1984. Using the Pagemaker app it was possible to create text on screen and print it out to a Laserwriter, the first printer based on the Postscript, Adobe's page description language.

Awkward combinations of letters that caused gaps in words could now be adjusted to fit together better (kerning) as the metal body no longer kept them apart. Although most typesetting was restricted to defined type sizes, they were more comprehensive than hot metal; the economy of space afforded by electronic font files resulted in greater ranges of typefaces becoming available from typesetters and printers.

And still technology and engineering marched on. In 1981, IBM launched the IBM Personal Computer (PC), the first small desktop computer with a text-based interface, responding to typed commands. In 1984, Apple Computers introduced the Macintosh computer. This was also a desktop machine, but it had a Graphical User Interface (GUI); an operating system that consisted of on-screen menus, windows, and icons that allowed the user to interact with the computer by pointing with a cursor via a "mouse."

In 1985, Apple joined forces with Adobe and Aldus to create a new branch of personal computer application. Adobe was a company formed to develop Postscript level 1, a page description language that was capable of controlling output devices such as laser printers and imagesetters, which was to become an industry standard. Aldus was a small new software company marketing PageMaker, a typesetting and layout program. Apple's part in this deal was to produce a laserwriter. Desktop publishing had arrived, ready to transform the world of printing and graphic design within the next decade.

Avove: Early desktop computers were largely rejected by typographers and graphic designers because of the low-resolution type generation. However, many designers relished the new imagery the computer could produce.

TWO RIVAL METHODS were developed for generating desktop computer fonts. Type 1 fonts were developed by Adobe and consisted of two parts: a set of fixed-size bitmap font files for screen display and a Postscript font file to be used by the output device.

Digital type formats

TrueType, the other method developed by Apple, provided information for screen and output device in a single file, sufficient to generate plain, plain italic, bold, and bold italic.

Most standard font character sets would contain up to 256 glyphs (characters), which consist of capitals and lowercase letters, figures, floating accents, common mathematical characters, reference symbols, currency symbols, and punctuation marks.

OPENTYPE

Adobe OpenType introduces major innovations to digital typesetting. First, it is a cross-platform: file format. Second it is supported by Unicode to provide an increase of the standard character set of up to 64,000 glyphs. The regular typeface can now include a far greater number of characters, ligatures, true small capitals, Old-style figures, swash capitals, fractions, and special characters, as well as Cyrillic and Greek making possible typographic designs of amazing refinement and richness never before achievable.

ZAPFINO

Zapfino is a showcase example of what the OpenType format has to offer the designer. Hermann Zapf's preoccupation with the hand-rendered forms of calligraphy, which could not

be satisfied fully by metal type technology, has now found fulfilment with digital technology. The script letterform is a variety of font that has notably benefited from digitization, no longer suffering from the limitations imposed by a metal body.

Full access to OpenType Zapfino Extra can only be achieved with applications that support OpenType; InDesign, Photoshop, Illustrator, and QuarkXpress. By using OpenType, Hermann Zapf has managed to take Zapfino beyond a digital script font into the realm of electronic calligraphy, normally only achievable by very skilled hands. The availability of such a large number of alternative characters and flourishes, in addition to the four related alphabets, has created an organic form that makes it possible to produce the same piece of copy in numerous different arrangements. Zapfino Extra constitutes a virtual calligraphy kit.

WEB OPEN TYPE FORMAT

Until recently web pages were resticted to "web safe" font ie those available on the endusers computer but nowadays designers have the freedom to use a wide variety of WOFF fonts that can be embedded in a web page without contravening copyright restrictions as the font cannot be reused elsewhere.

Titling
Titling

Right: Enabling the Fractions feature in the OpenType sub-menu allows software to recognize sequences such as "½," and automatically match them to fraction glyphs in the font, if available.

1/2 ½

2/3 ⅔

Some OpenType fonts include alternative glyphs for use as titles, using the Titling Alternates option. The upper title here is set as Titling Alternates—the effect is subtle.

Right: Tabular numbers occupy a fixed width, making it easy to align them vertically. Proportional numbers act like ordinary typeset text, with varying character widths. The example here shows a math book sum set as proportional (right) and as tabular (far right).

$$137 + 364 = 501$$

$$137 + 364 = 501$$

Right: Even using the basic character a font like Zapfino would have been an impractical proposition before the advent of OpenType.

abcdefghijklmnopqrstuvwxyz&

ABCDEFGHIJKLMN
OPQRSTUVWXYZ

Biggest
Flogged

Left: Zapfino Extra provides alternative glyphs for a particular character depending upon context, such as whether it begins or ends a word, or what other characters are next to it. The sophistication of this is apparent in the styling of the pairs of "g"s in the words on the left.

DESPITE THE MANY radical changes in the printing industry over the last 40 years, many of the old terms have lingered on, even if the technologies have not. Digital technology has maintained the evocative term "foundry" for the organizations originating typefaces for computers.

Digital type foundries

8

Monotype and Linotype hold many of the greatest 20th-century revivals of classic typefaces, from the 15th-century Jenson to Franklin Gothic from the 20th century. The introduction of desktop computing stimulated the formation of many new companies to provide digital typefaces.

ADOBE

A Californian company, Adobe has played a major role in the success of computer-generated graphic design and typography. Through joint marketing agreements made in the early 1990s, Adobe, Linotype, and Monotype started selling one another's fonts as well as their own.

Adobe now has a font library of at least 2,500 fonts, including those designed by an in-house design team that has included Sumner Stone, Robert Slimbach, and Carol Twombly.

BITSTREAM

Bitstream Inc. was the first independent digital typefoundry, formed in 1981. The Bitstream Library contains over 1,000 fonts, which include many of the revived classicss—all digitized and hinted to Bitstream's own standards.

EMIGRE

Emigre Fonts was another of the early independent digital typefoundries. Emigre first appeared

as a magazine designed and published by husband and wife team Rudy VanderLans and Zuzana Licko. Both were students who had arrived at the time when the first Macintosh personal computer came onto the market and New Wave typography was gaining ground.

Emigre, more than any other digital typefoundry, has taken on from the start the challenge of the Macintosh computer to traditional concepts of type design. Zuzana Licko started her career as a type designer in the 1980s, experimenting with the 72-dots-per-inch computer screen to create digital fonts that accepted the limits of low-resolution bitmap formats for use on dot-matrix printers. Since 1985, she has been responsible for over 36 typefaces, including Filosophia (1996), a tribute to Giambattista Bodoni, and Mrs Eaves (1996), a tribute to John Baskerville; these can be considered as new digital revivals, expressing the essence of the original historic typefaces rather than creating an authentic remastering.

FONTFONT

In 1989, Erik Spiekermann and Neville Brody set up FontShop International, a supplier of digital typefaces for the expanding numbers of designers turning to the new technology. Erik Spiekermann was a founder member of the

Officina was designed by Erik Spiekermann and Ole Schäfer. It is a sans-serif and serif form reminiscent of typewriter face and was originally intended for inter-office correspondence.

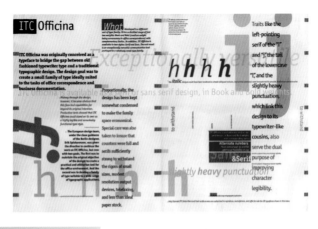

Designed by Lucas de Groot, Thesis has three main styles, the serif, the sans, and the mix. Each style has a range of weights from extra light to black in roman and italics plus small capitals; this results in 144 related alphabets.

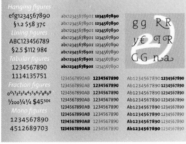

Meta is a sans-serif developed by Erik Spiekermann and named after his studio, MetaDesign in Berlin. Meta is a digital sans-serif, and it introduced a new friendly quality influencing many other digital sans-serifs.

Berlin-based design group MetaDesign. He became a germinal figure in typographic design at a time when the New Wave was moving into excess. His characteristically witty books on the practice of typography, including *Stop Stealing Sheep* (1993), was pivotal in redefining the principles of typographic communication. Among the original fonts in his FontFont collection is Spiekermann's Meta, released 1991, one of the earliest sans-serifs designed as a digital type, and Lucas de Groot's Thesis, which is almost a font collection in itself. It takes the family concept to the ultimate; with three forms, a delicate slab-serif, a semi-serif, and sans-serif, and with eight weights and italics, it offers a total of 144 font variants.

2

ANATOMY OF TYPE

THERE ARE TWO fundamental aspects of the anatomy of type that dictate how we utilize it. The first is the somewhat mechanical and practical aspect of its physical dimensions, the methods by which it is constructed and the units by which we measure it both horizontally and vertically.

Type components

9

We need to know from which point a letter, word, or line is measured, and what the terms governing the measurement system are, so that on a practical level we can make our typesetting software do what we ask of it. The second is the shape, construction, and visual appearance of individual letterforms. Being able to name the type parts that make up a character's unique quality gives us a language through which to express our opinions, evaluations, and judgments.

Much of the terminology we use today comes from the days of letterpress printing. Characters were in those days constructed on a physical "body" or piece of metal. The dimensions of the body included the distance from the top of the tallest ascender in the type to the bottom of the lowest descender, plus a small amount of extra space, which varied from type to type. The extra

space or "body clearance" ensured that, when type was set solid (without extra line spacing), there was no danger that ascenders and descenders would touch each other if an ascender happens to fall below a descender. Body size is the same as type size, our current term.

"Cap height" is the height of the capital letter. It should be noted that, in many cases, this is not the same height as the ascenders in a given typeface: it is usually slightly less than the ascender height.

All letters sit on a "baseline," with descenders falling below. The baseline position is of great significance because it is the point from which all digital typesetting software measures the relative vertical position of type. Line spacing (commonly now called "leading") is calculated from baseline to baseline.

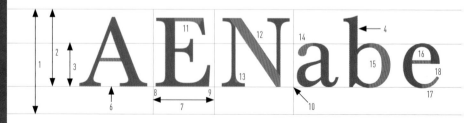

A key measurement in lowercase letters is the x-height, the height of a lower case x. It is the x-height that largely dictates the tonal value of lines of type. Paradoxically, although ascenders or descenders provide a certain quirkiness and individuality that helps us to recognize letter shapes and word formations quickly when seen at a glance in a body of text, they contribute little to the grayness value or tonal value. The x-height provides that.

From typeface to typeface, the ratios of type size to cap height and x-height, and of cap height and x-height to each other, will not be constant. One typeface set in 12 point may not have the same x-height or cap height as a different type-face set in 12 point. This means that letters in one type may be bigger or smaller than in an-other type of the same size. The result is that the number of characters in any given line length will change from type to type. Switching from one type to another, even at the same point size, will very rarely provide identical line endings. Usually, a change in type will result in either fewer or more lines.

Different x-heights change the relationship of black ink to white page, so that same-sized fonts with different x-heights will produce different tonal values on a page. This could be a critical factor in selecting a typeface.

Above: Typefaces can have different proportions within the same body height (i.e. type size).

Below: The components that make up one letter are common to other letters in the same type. When repeated constantly throughout a piece of setting, they become characteristics, giving it an overall flavor and feel. The angle of any inclined stress, the relative widths of thick and thin strokes, the proportion of the x-height, and serif shape are just a few examples of common letter components that make up the overall quality of a typeface.

Type parts

1	Body
2	Cap height
3	x-height
4	Ascender
5	Descender
6	Baseline
7	Body width
8	Left sidebearing
9	Right sidebearing
10	Character origin
11	Arm
12	Stroke
13	Bracket
14	Ball
15	Bowl
16	Hairline
17	Terminal
18	Finial
19	Spur
20	Serif
21	Link
22	Ear
23	Link
24	Bar
25	Counter
26	Stem
27	Spine

THE TERM TYPEFACE did not emerge until after the invention of moveable type in the 15th century. The early designs were strongly influenced by the hand-drawn calligraphic letterforms that preceded them and in particular the Blackletter or Gothic style exemplified by Textura and it was on this that Gutenberg based his early typefaces.

Type classification

The Blackletter form was eventually superseded by what we now know as the Roman style with its familiar serifs that was based on Classical Roman capitals but with the addition of minuscules or lower case as they were known later.

This design has undergone continuous evolution during the last five centuries and many attempts have been made to classify them into a coherent family tree. Classification has been problematic, as in common with all creative endeavors, designers borrowed from each other as knowledge of printing and type styles quickly spread across all of Europe. However, certain characteristics are common among type styles resulting in a broadly accepted nomenclature that was later expanded to include sans serif styles: Humanist, Old Style, Transitional, Didone, Slab Serif (Egyptian), Sans-Serif, Calligraphic.

The evolution of these styles, particularly the five serif genres, was influenced by developments in printing, type manufacturing, and paper making technology. As these improved it was possible to produce ever finer type designs that gave a lighter color to the printed page.

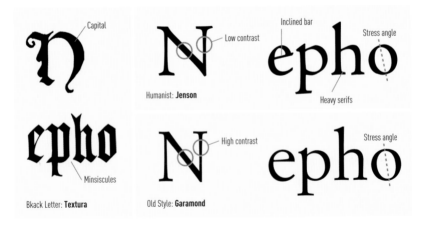

Capital

Minsiscules

Bkack Letter: **Textura**

Humanist: **Jenson**

Low contrast

Old Style: **Garamond**

High contrast

Inclined bar

Stress angle

Heavy serifs

Stress angle

HUMANIST

The Humanist style developed in Venice in the 15th century and sought to imitate the formal handwriting of the Carolingian minuscule, popular during the reign of Charlemagne. It characterized as being fairly heavy in color with a small x-height, strong, bracketed serifs, some with an angled thrust, a strongly angled stress and often with a square full point. The bar on the lowercase "e" is usually sharply inclined. They have a low contrast between the thickest and thinnest parts of the character design.

THE OLD STYLE (GARALDE)

Lighter in color than Humanist styles with bracketed serifs and less extreme angle of character stress. They have slightly more contrast between the thickest and thinnest parts of the character design, most noticeable between downstroke and upstroke on capitals.

The term Garalde derives from a combination of the names of type designers Claude Garamond and Aldus Manutius.

TRANSITIONAL

As the name suggests this style forms a transition between Old Style and Didone (Modern) that appeared some 250 years later. The angle of character stress is almost vertical and the contrast between the thickest and thinnest parts of the character design has increased even more.

DIDONE (MODERN)

This style can be characterized as having hairline unbracketed serifs and a completely vertical thrust. They have a very high contrast between the thickest and thinnest parts of the character design most noticeable on capitals. The term Didone derives from a combination of the names François Didot and Giambattista Bodoni

SLAB SERIF

Slab Serif (Egyptian) is a geometric style that has thick unbracketed serifs that do not taper at all. They have vertical stress. There is usually no contrast between the thickest and thinnest parts of the character design.

Transitional: **Bulmer**

Stress angle

Didone: **Didot**

Very high contrast

Stress angle

Hairline serifs

No contrast

Serifs don't taper

Slab Serif: **Rockwell**

Type classification

9

SANS-SERIF (LINEAL)

This typestyle has several sub categories that include: Grotesque, Neo-grotesque, Geometric, and Humanist.

GROTESQUE

Grotesque were the first sans serif typefaces and originated in the 19th century. There is usually some degree of contrast between the thickest and thinnest parts of the character design, characterized by inward curving strokes on characters like C and S. The terminals of curves are usually horizontal. They often have a spur on the "g" and the "R" usually has a curved leg

NEO-GROTESQUE

This style emerged in the 20th century. They have a very regular design and have very little

Curved leg
Spur on g
Terminals close to horizontal
Double storey g

Grotesque: **Bureau Grot**

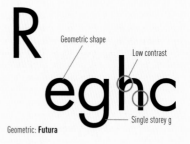

Geometric shape
Low contrast
Single storey g

Geometric: **Futura**

Terminal slanted
Single storey g

Neo-Grotesque: **Akzidenz Grotesk**

Open counters
Low contrast
Double storey g

Humanist Sans Serif: **Gill Sans**

contrast between the thickest and thinnest parts of the character design, and the terminals of curves are usually slanted.

GEOMETRIC

These are constructed using often repeated simple geometric shapes and have very little contrast between the thickest and thinnest parts of the character design.

HUMANIST (SANS-SERIF)

Characterized by open counters on characters like C and S the Humanist style of sans-serif draws its inspiration from the Humanist serif design rather than from the 19th century Grotesque sans-serif faces

CALLIGRAPHIC

There is too wide a range of Calligraphic styles to be able to define many universal characteristics. The only common factor is that they mimic pen and brush drawn or engraved letterforms. There are however some generally agreed sub-categories: Glyphic (engraved), Formal Script, Informal Script, and Gaelic.

The classification of type styles created during the digital era is near impossible as there are so many and the influences upon their designers so diverse. However many of the more serious type designers of today are keen to explain the lineage of their creations in order to afford them some historic perspective and to help those who will research this subject in the future.

"Engraved" serifs

Open counters

Calligraphic Glyphic: **Trajan**

Small x-height

Pen drawn

Calligraphic Formal Script: **Bickham**

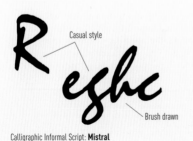

Casual style

Brush drawn

Calligraphic Informal Script: **Mistral**

Capitals are same size as miniscules

Broad pen drawn

Calligraphic Uncial: **Uncial**

A TYPE'S INDIVIDUALITY depends on dozens of subtle characteristics, particularly the forms of special strokes and special letters. Some letters look very similar in many types, especially if they are from the same type category—the lowercase letters "l" or "o" for example, or even the "H."

"God" is in the detail

Some letters to look for, when studying typefaces, are g, a, r, and Q. These letters are subject to many variations of detailing by type designers, since they readily lend themselves to varied forms of interpretation. The variations of these key letterforms are thus useful when identifying typefaces that may, at first glance, look identical. Another outstanding character is the ampersand, &. A beautifully crafted ampersand can lend grace and beauty to a page. Many is the time that choice of typeface been made solely on the design of its ampersand. Conversely, many a good-looking typeface has been spoilt by an ugly ampersand.

TYPE CATEGORIES

Traditional type categories are useful in that they provide us with a sense of historical development but, more importantly, they enable us to develop notions of broadly similar stylistic treatment in typeface design. Each category is characterized by general similarities of structure and form that help us to identify type. Types that fall into the same category will share many common attributes, and it is always useful, when discussing or selecting type, to have a form of shorthand to which to refer. As we may distinguish between schools of artistic development such as, say, Art Nouveau or Art Deco, so too we

may distinguish between phases in stylistic trends and landmarks in typefaces design.

Mies van der Rohe once wrote, on the subject of architecture, that "God is in the detail." His little maxim must have been quoted thousands of times by design educators ever since. Nowhere is this more true than in typographic design. Typography is entirely about the business of detailing. Typesetting is now the responsibility of the graphic designer and this has brought advantages and disadvantages. The obvious advantages are speed and economy: the luxury of being able to dispense with casting-off tables, to change one's mind at will, to create special effects, to have control over spacing issues, and (though not a typographic issue) to do it all without the craft skill of "paste-up." A major disadvantage is that it very quickly shows up the lack of accurate detailing skills possessed by many designers. Much subtle detailing used to be routinely taken care of by expert typesetters or compositors who had followed rigorous apprenticeships. Consistent, correct punctuation was supplied by the compositor, as was the correct use of ellipses, em dashes, asterisks, daggers, spaces after full stops, and sensible hyphenation. Much of this attention to detail was either not recognized or not appreciated by graphic designers.

Typeface recognition can often be difficult when typefaces appear superficially similar. Certain letters (characters) have a more individual form than others and it is the detailing of these that often gives you clues for easier recognition. Look at the lowercase g, a, r, and q, or the capital "Q." The design of the capital "G" is often a telltale sign in sans-serif faces.

1 Baskerville
2 Goudy Old Style
3 Centaur
4 Caslon 540
5 Baker Signet
6 Bodoni Book
7 Century Light
8 Gill sans
9 News Gothic Light

The Caslon italic ampersand is one of the most prominent characters in typography but the design varies in different version of the face. Top row: Caslon 3, Caslon 540, Adobe Caslon Pro, and below ITC Caslon with Swashes.

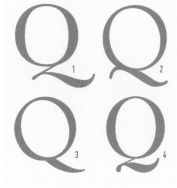

IN ADDITION TO the basic character set common to most fonts, many include extra glyphs in the extended character set and this is particularly so since the advent of OpenType, which allows for 65,000 individual characters. Others offer a separate font that includes these as well as non aligning numerals and ligatures in an "Expert Set."

Expert sets

Expert Set fonts provide alternative numerals, known as Old Style or non-lining numerals, parts of which rise above or fall below the baseline. Apart from being beautiful characters in their own right, they provide useful distinction when the numerals 1 and 0 are in close proximity to the capital letters I and O. Most Expert Sets also contain small capitals, crafted to match both the x-height and its tonal value. Small capitals can be produced by scaling down normal capitals, but they are always too thin. Some typefaces have been designed with alternate characters, perhaps more ornate or with swashes. These are also found in Expert Sets.

Set at display sizes, many special symbols such as ® and © look far too big: they look better when reduced to the size of running text and raised ("shifted") from the baseline. Some fonts (e.g. ITC Officina) come with such symbols already reduced and raised.

Poor punctuation is generally a result of inconsistent authorship and subsequent setting. A proliferation of unnecessary commas, mixed colons and semi colons, and incorrect use of single and double quotation marks easily mars a good run of text, and is particularly annoying after you have lavished time and care over all the other aspects of aesthetic detailing. Inconsistent use of en and em dashes, brackets and parentheses also breaks up the textural rhythm, thereby spoiling an otherwise clean piece of setting.

Most fonts contain properly designed quotation marks and most major design applications have "smart quotes" features to allow them to be used easily. But all too often one sees instead the use of "tick marks," i.e. ' and "—usually used to denote feet and inches. The type designer will have carefully and lovingly designed real quotation marks to match the style of his typeface: they should be always used. Some applications allow automatic "smart quotes" to be switched off: make sure that everyone who processes your work (e.g. editors and printers) has the software configured to your specification.

Control of character and word spacing, line and paragraph spacing will be discussed on the following pages. But it would be right to make it clear here that only one word space is used after a full point, and not two. "Type two spaces after a full point" was drummed into generations of typists because for monospaced typewriting it improved clarity. But professional typesetters, who have always worked with proportionally spaced characters, have always used just one space after a full point. Now that all computer users work with proportionally spaced letters, they should follow suit in order to avoid unsightly and inconsistent spacing.

abcdefghijklmnop
qrstuvwxyz
ABCDEFGHIJKLMN
OPQRSTUVWXYZ
1234567890

Scala Regular

Left: Scala is an elegant serif font designed in 1989 by Martin Majoor. In common with many contemporary fonts its uses non aligning numerals as standard and includes regular numerals in an Expert set along with Euro symbol that is now included in the regular font.

Below: The remainder of the character set includes punctuation, fractions, accented characters (diacritics), symbols, and ligatures.

€◇◇◆◁▷≤≥
⌄⌃~−◡··· ¤≈I

1234567890

Scala Caps Exp

ABCDEFGHI
JKLMNOPQR
STUVWXYZ

Scala Caps

!"#$%&'()*+,-./:;<=>?@[\]
^_`{|}~¡¢£¤¥¦§¨©ª«¬
®¯°±²³´µ¶·¹⁰»¼½¾¿
ÀÁÂÃÄÅÆÇÈÉÊËÌÍÎÏÐÑ
ÒÓÔÕÖØÙÚÛÜÝÞß
àáâãäåæçèéëìíïïðñòóôõö÷
øùúûüýþÿıłŁŒœŠšŸŽžƒ
ˆˇ˘˙˚˛˜˝‗‘’‚“”„†‡•…
‰‹›/€™–fifl

The ripe fig is SWEET to taste...

A ligature replaces the "fi" in the word fig. Small caps, designed to fit within the x-height but the same weight as the lower case letters, is used for emphasis without interuption the flow of the text.

PARAGRAPHS ARE THE essential building blocks of running text. Without paragraph breaks, text would be very difficult to read, so it follows that we should pay special attention to how paragraphs are formed. The designer should question and make decisions about the following paragraph features before any setting takes place.

Anatomy of a paragraph

9

- Column width
- Font
- Size
- Weight
- Style (roman, italic)
- Case (uppercase, large and small caps or upper and lowercase)
- Line spacing (leading)
- Character spacing (tracking)
- Paragraph spacing
- Alignment (ranged left, ranged right, centered, or justified)
- First-line indents or hanging indents
- Hanging punctuation
- Raised or dropped initial capitals
- Hyphenation

Quite a lot to think about! We cannot allow decisions on these matters to go by default for all aspects of paragraph design will have a profound effect on tone, texture, page coloring, and overall effectiveness of our work.

Right: This example shows how a double space after a full point makes an unnecessary gap in the flow of a piece of text. Justifying text across a narrow column can create over-narrow or over-wide character spacing. A hyphen has also been used in place of an en or em dash, either of which would have been more elegant.

Hyphen

Fellow countrymen-Four score and seven years ago our fathers brought forth on this continent a new nation, conceived in liberty, and dedicated to the proposition that all men are created equal.

Tight space

Now we are engaged in a great civil war, testing whether that nation, or any nation so conceived and so dedicated, can long endure. We are met on a great battlefield of that war. We have come to dedicate a portion of that field as a final resting-place for those who here gave their lives that that nation might live. It is altogether fit and proper that we should do this.

Open space

Double space

"**F**ellow countrymen – Four score and seven years ago our fathers brought forth on this continent a new nation, conceived in liberty, and dedicated to the proposition that all men are created equal.

Now we are engaged in a great civil war, testing whether that nation, or any nation so conceived and so dedicated, can long endure. We are met on a great battlefield of that war. We have come to dedicate a portion of that field as a final resting-place for those who here gave their lives that that nation might live. It is altogether fit and proper that we should do this.

But, in a larger sense, we cannot dedicate – we cannot consecrate – we cannot hallow this ground. The brave men, living and dead, who struggled here, have consecrated it, far above our poor power to add or detract. The world will little note, nor long remember, what we say here, but it can never forget what they did here. It is for us, the living, rather, to dedicated here to the unfinished work which they who fought here have thus far so nobly advanced. It is rather for us to be here dedicated to the great task remaining before us – that from these honoured dead we take increased devotion to that cause for which they gave the last full measure of devotion – that we here highly resolve that these dead shall not have died in vain – that this nation, under God, shall have a new birth of freedom – and that government of the people, by the people, for the people, shall not perish from the earth. "

ABRAHAM LINCOLN
Gettysburg, 19 November 1863

THE DESIGN OF LETTERFORMS is of primary concern to the type designer but so too is the relationship between pairs of characters and the space between them. So before we consider modifying, to any degree, the character spacing for any font, we need to be aware of its standard or default characteristics.

Kerning and tracking

9

Many aspects of spacing are interrelated; an alteration to one set of controls may well have a knock-on effect with others, which can be initially bewildering. The best way to understand what is going on is to examine each of these in isolation. How each may interact with the others can then be better assessed.

HORIZONTAL SPACING CONTROL

Horizontal spacing is achieved through character and word spacing. Typographers, typesetters, graphic designers, and publishers have always wanted some control over how character spacing behaves. There are many reasons for this, and every type practitioner will have an individual view about how much of this is desirable. Despite the significant time, energy, attention to detail, and love that go into designing a type, it is virtually impossible for the typeface designer to cater for the countless variations of use and the situations in which the type may be employed.

TRACKING

Tracking is the term for the spacing between characters in a range or run of text. It should not be confused with kerning, which relates only to the adjustment of space between individual pairs of characters. Tracking may be applied in several ways, and how it is applied varies from one

software package to another. Each character has a given width, determined by the type designer, which includes very small amounts of space on each side of the glyph, called the "side-bearings." The side-bearings ensure that, when text is set to the default, ideal standard envisaged by the type designer, the characters do not touch. When a range of characters is assembled normally, so that only the side-bearings provide the white space between them, the tracking value is described as "0" (zero). We can depart from this norm by taking away a fractional space between each character or by adding it. This produces the effect of closer- or looser-spaced characters.

It is because these adjustments involve tiny amounts of space that the old system of points and ems is still used by today's type designers, typographers, and computer systems. At approximately 0.35 mm, even one point is too large to be used as an increment of spacing small sizes of type, so a much finer unit is derived from it.

A little thought will also quickly show that for very large sizes of type one point might be too small an increment. What we need is a very small unit that varies relative to the type size. This unit is one-thousandth (0.001) of an em, where the em (unlike the pica em, which is always 12 points) is the same as the type size. In 10 pt type the em is 10 points, and all character

Left: As the spacing between the two letters is produced purely by their sidebearing, the letterspacing is considered to have a value of 0.

Sidebearings

Track 0

Left: Tracking of 10 opens up the distance between letters.

Track 10

Above: The kerning pair for cap "WA" shows negative sidebearing in order to avoid visually uneven spacing.

spacing is based on thousandths of 10 points. Likewise, 7 pt type will use units of thousandths of 7 points. This is a microscopic unit, but as type size changes it remains optically constant. When tracking has been decreased, it is shown as a negative number (e.g. –7); when it is increased, it is shown as a positive number (e.g. 7).

The standard word space is a width determined by the font designer and is individual to each typeface, although in many cases it approximates to half or one-third of the em. Word spaces are also affected by changes in tracking values across a range of text.

Tracking should be changed for aesthetic reasons. Small type, for instance, may begin to look too tight, resulting in diminished legibility. A small global increase to the tracking values may improve the overall look and ease of reading.

KERNING

The spacing between individual pairs of letters is called kerning. Whereas tracking values control a range of characters, kerning explicitly refers to the extra space placed uniquely between two specified characters.

Some pairs of characters, when spaced out uniformly, do not always sit comfortably together, e.g. Wa, WA, Tr, and so on. Font designers take these anomalies into account when designing typefaces by building kerning tables that work in the background, taking fractions of space away or adding it appropriately as letters are combined, resulting in more pleasing character relationships, e.g. Wa, WA, Tr, and so on. It is important to note that, since kerning tables are built into the font metrics, any further manually applied kerning will be added or subtracted. So when the cursor is placed between W and A, a kerning value of 0 (zero) is registered.

DESIGN SOFTWARE PACKAGES offer methods by which the user may specify how and under what conditions automatic hyphenation will occur. They all, furthermore, offer the option of having no hyphenation at all, unless it is keyed in manually.

Justification and hyphenation

9

Justification means that text is set so that both left and right line endings range to a given paragraph width, so the amount of space between words will inevitably be variable unless hyphenation is used.

The calculations used to assess break-points for hyphenation depend on the software knowing precise line lengths. Justification decisions are calculated on the basis of whether hyphenation is desired or not, and to what extent the spaces within a line may be stretched or compressed. It will thus be seen that these two controls are very much interrelated. Typographers must consider hyphenation and justification as one issue; this is why the term "H&J" is widely used to embrace these key aspects of typesetting.

JUSTIFICATION

To understand justification, it is best to look first at what happens when type is set unjustified. As each character is keyed, it is placed after the previous one according to the standard spacing values contained in the font file. Each word is followed by the standard word space designed for that font. When a word is added to a line that is almost full, the software assesses whether there is room for it. If there is not, it will be forced onto the next line, leaving the line before slightly short. All this will take into account any kerning

and tracking values that have been altered. The characters and their accompanying word spaces will look uniform and generally pleasing, but the right edge of the block of text will be ragged because the line lengths are uneven.

Justification aims to make all lines in a block of text end in the same place. As before, words and spaces are assembled on a line from left to right, and when a word is added to a line that is almost full the software assesses whether there is room for it. If there is not, the software quickly assesses two choices. Every word space on the line could be reduced to accommodate the word, or the word could be pushed onto the following line and the word spaces that are already on the line could be increased in order to fill the entire line length.

So that justification may be carried out successfully, the software uses certain routines in sequence to calculate the best choice. The best choice is that which provides the most uniform and satisfactory visual effect. Tightening up some word spaces may allow a word to be fitted on a line, but too much tightening will result in the word spaces becoming too small. So the software refers to a numerical limit beyond which word spacing may not be decreased; this limit is the minimum word space. Once this limit is reached, the software can only fit the word on the line if it reduces the space between characters. This is also subject to a limit: the minimum character spacing. If the software fails to fit it on the line, the word is pushed at last onto the next line. Reverting to the line it was working on, the software has now to increase the word spacing to spread the words evenly across the column width. Again, for the sake of aesthetics, this increase is subject to a limit beyond which no more space may be added; this limit is the maximum word space. Once this limit is reached, the software can only fill out the line if it increases the space between characters. This is also subject to a limit: the maximum character spacing.

The whole process of justification depends on the software using minimum, "normal," and maximum values for spacing of both words and characters. It must be remembered that, in determining any need for adjustment, the design software addresses these values in sequence—first word spacing, followed by character spacing. Remember, however, that all calculations will take into account any change to kerning and tracking values you have made.

The whole objective of this process is to achieve lines of type that are justified (i.e. flush on both left and right) but do not appear to be unduly squashed or spread out, thereby producing an even and constant textural color. This is not always possible, and consequently there are situations where unsatisfactory and ugly gaps, called rivers, appear in a body of text, spoiling its overall appearance. This occurs most often when columns are narrow.

"A free America, democratic in the sense that our forefathers intended it to be, means just this: individual freedom for all, rich or poor, or else this system of government we call democracy is only an expedient to enslave man to the machine and make him like it."
Frank Lloyd Wright

"A free America, democratic in the sense that our forefathers intended it to be, means just this: individual freedom for all, rich or poor, or else this system of government we call democracy is only an expedient to enslave man to the machine and make him like it."
Frank Lloyd Wright

"A free America, democratic in the sense that our forefathers intended it to be, means just this: individual freedom for all, rich or poor, or else this system of government we call democracy is only an expedient to enslave man to the machine and make him like it."
Frank Lloyd Wright

Above left: Ranged left text has even word spacing. Justification creates neat blocks of text but brings its own problems—particularly to narrow measures. Above center: Over-spacing and over-tightening inevitably occur in achieving evenly flush line ends. Above right: Hyphenation (word breaking) goes some way to alleviating this problem but is not always completely successful.

HYPHENATION MAY BE USED for justified or unjustified text, and the hyphens may be inserted manually or automatically. When applied to ranged left text it is used to control the variation of line lengths (shape of the "rag"). In justified setting its purpose is to eliminate too much or too little word spacing.

Hyphenation for unjustified text

9

When a long word is forced onto a new line leaving an unduly large space at the end of the line, manually typing a hyphen in the word will break it and allow the part before the hyphen to return and lengthen the preceding line. A danger of typing such a hyphen manually is that, if the text reflows owing to editorial or layout changes, the hyphen will travel with the word and may appear in the middle of a line. To avoid this problem, it is always advisable to type a "discretionary hyphen"

(command+shift+hyphen in Adobe InDesign). This is an invisible command that instructs the software to break the word and insert a hyphen if the word happens to fall at the end of the line.

The same keyboard commands entered at the start of a word, will prevent it from being hyphenated when auto-hyphenation is switched on. This is useful if breaking a word (e.g. a name) is undesirable. Adobe InDesign calls this a non-breaking command.

A hotel is a place that keeps the makers of 25-watt bulbs in business.	A hotel is a place that keeps the makers of 25-watt bulbs in business.	If a politician found he had cannibals among his many constituents, he would promise them missionaries for dinner.	If a politician found he had cannibals among his many con-stituents, he would promise them missionaries for dinner.
Shelly Berman	Shelly Berman	H. L. Mencken	H. L. Mencken

Above: Some composite words are already hyphenated. To ensure that they do not break and acquire an extra hyphen, it is best to key a non-breaking hyphen.

Above: Where there is a very short line shown above, it is useful to insert a discretionary hyphen. This will break the word but should it appear elsewhere due to later editorial changes, the hyphen will disappear.

PARAGRAPH COMPOSER

InDesign uses the Paragraph Composer by default. It considers all the breakpoints in an entire paragraph, and thus can optimize earlier lines in the paragraph in order to eliminate especially unattractive breaks later on. Paragraph composition results in more even spacing with fewer hyphens. The Single Line Composer can be used as an alternative.

HYPHENATION ZONE

The hyphenation zone is another way of controlling the shape of the "rag"; it permits further refinement in the process of auto-hyphenation of unjustified text by exerting some control over the raggedness of the right margin. When auto-hyphenation is switched on but no hyphenation zone is specified, the last word in an unjustified line will be hyphenated according to the normal rules that determine word-breaks if it is too long to fit. The result is often that the lines are of more even length but also that they display an abundance of hyphens. If we were prepared to have less evenness in the line endings, we would need fewer hyphens. The hyphenation zone allows us to specify this choice. The zone is measured inward from the right side of the column, and its width in effect tells the software that no hyphenation is required as long as the line ends within the zone. If an unhyphenated word ends within the zone, the next word will not be broken, even if it could be hyphenated before the end of the line. If it is too long, it will simply be forced onto the next line. If a potentially hyphenated word coincides with the start of the hyphenation zone, or begins to its left, it will be broken. The use of hyphenation zones thus makes line lengths vary more (look more ragged) whilst reducing the incidence of hyphens. In unjustified typesetting, this feature provides an extremely useful method of controlling the contour, and therefore shape, of column edges.

The English country gentleman galloping after a fox; the unspeakable in full pursuit of the uneatable.

Oscar Wilde

The English country gentleman galloping after a fox; the unspeakable in full pursuit of the uneatable.

Oscar Wilde

The English country gentleman galloping after a fox; the unspeakable in full pursuit of the uneatable.

Oscar Wilde

The English country gentleman galloping after a fox; the unspeakable in full pursuit of the uneatable.

Oscar Wilde

Above from left to right: no hyphenation, hyphenation on, hyphenation limited to one. Again a discretionary hyphen would work best here.

Above: This paragraph has 12mm hyphenation zone

THE TECHNIQUE OF MANUALLY inserting hyphens is the same as for unjustified text, and it is again advisable to use discretionary hyphens. Non-breaking hyphens may be inserted in the same way as for unjustified text. As wide columns contain more word spaces the need for hyphenation is reduced.

Hyphenation for justified text

In narrow measures the need to hyphenate words becomes all the more necessary as opportunities for spreading or tightening are diminished. Although the hyphenation of a word does not unduly upset our ability to read, too many hyphenations mar the visual feel of a piece of text, so it is always the aim of a good designer to minimize the amount of hyphenation.

H&J CHECKLIST

CHANGE THE DEFAULT VALUE IF:
- The default settings produce unsatisfactory hyphenation.
- You want to permit more character spacing rather than word spacing.
- You want to permit more word spacing rather than character spacing.
- You need to resolve problems caused by a high incidence of either long or short words.
- You want to minimize the amount of hyphenation.
- You prefer to increase the amount of hyphenation to maintain better text color.

REMEMBER:
- Wide measures reduce the need to hyphenate; however, narrow measures increase the number of words needing to

AUTO-HYPHENATION
Automatic hyphenation is designed to produce the most satisfying results for most situations. As in the justification routines, hyphenation initially works according to the set of values that come as a default with the design software.

The software allows you to set values for the minimum number of characters a word must be hyphenated.
- Reduced tracking darkens the perceived tonal value of text on a page.
- Unhyphenated, ranged-left text will produce a more exaggerated raggedness on the right margin.
- Narrow measures of justified text are more likely to produce more white rivers.
- Excessive latitude in minimum and maximum word space values exaggerates the amount of word space.
- Little latitude in minimum and maximum word space values combined with too much latitude in character spacing results in words that appear to run into one another.
- The optimum word space value refers default fixed word space in unjustified text. Percentage relates to a percentage of the word-space size set in the font file.

Those parts of the system that you can hit with a hammer (not advised) are called hardware; those program instructions that you can only curse at are called software.

Author unknown

Those parts of the system that you can hit with a hammer (not advised) are called hardware; those program instructions that you can only curse at are called software.

Author unknown

+4 Those parts of the system that you can hit
+40 with a hammer (not
+70 advised) are called
+80 hardware; those pro-
+40 gram instructions that
+10 you can only curse at
+30 are called software.
+20

Author unknown

Above left to right:
H & J off;
H & J Standard;
H & J off with line-by-line tracking.

Plus or minus tracking values, line by line, can greatly enhance narrow columns by increasing the space between characters to harmonize

with those between words. This is practical only with small amounts of text as it is extremely labor-intensive.

contain for it to be auto-hyphenated and for the number of characters allowed before and after the hyphen. You can also specify whether words starting with capital letters (e.g. names) may be auto-hyphenated, and specify how many lines in sequence may end with a hyphen.

H & J WORKING TOGETHER

Hyphenation decisions, automatic or manual, are made only after the software has referred to the optimum, maximum, or minimum values to check whether difficult words may be accommodated on a line in order to achieve a reasonable result. If this fails, the hyphenation process takes over—according to either manual input, or to auto-hyphenation, in accordance with the hyphenation values.

Automated decision-making doesn't mean that we need worry how hyphenation or justification works. There are too many idiosyncratic demands arising from text assembly and too many conditions under which finished work may be viewed for any standard values to work con-

sistently well. Poor hyphenation inevitably gives text an unsatisfactory appearance. The more control we have over word-breaking, the better our chance we have of producing even, satisfying text matter.

INDESIGN HYPHENATION SETTINGS

Words with at Least. This will ignore short words. If you don't want short words to break set this to 5 or higher.

After First. The minumum number of characters of the word fragment preceding a hyphen.

Before Last. The minumum number of characters of the word fragment following a hyphen. In order to avoid "ly" for example by itself on a line set this to at least three.

Hyphen Limit. Set a limit to the number of consecutive hyphens you'll allow.

Hyphenation Zone. This is an invisble zone on the right hand side. If the word before the potentially hyphenated word falls inside the zone InDesign pushes the word onto the next line without hyphenating it.

THE COLOR AND TEXTURE of text will also be affected by the choice of vertical line spacing. As lines of type are moved apart, more white space on the page is revealed, thus lightening the body of text. As lines get closer, so the text becomes denser and darker. Clearly some good control over how this is achieved would be useful.

Leading

9

Line space is controlled by leading values, usually expressed in points. In modern usage, the term leading means the distance from the baseline of one line of type to the baseline of the next, which includes both the type and any extra space added. (The old usage meant only the extra space.) Some software allows you to specify a mode of leading, either "word-processing" or "typographic"; always choose "typographic." In most software, the default value for leading is

A human being is a part of the whole, called by us Universe, a part limited in time and space. He experiences himself, his thoughts and feelings as something separated from the rest, a kind of optical delusion of his consciousness. This delusion is a kind of prison, restricting us to our personal desires and to affection for a few persons nearest to us. Our task must be to free from this prison by widening our circle of compassion to embrace all living creatures and the whole nature in its beauty.
Albert Einstein

7/7 point

A human being is a part of the whole, called by us Universe, a part limited in time and space. He experiences himself, his thoughts and feelings as something separated from the rest, a kind of optical delusion of his consciousness. This delusion is a kind of prison, restricting us to our personal desires and to affection for a few persons nearest to us. Our task must be to free from this prison by widening our circle of compassion to embrace all living creatures and the whole nature in its beauty.
Albert Einstein

7/8.4 point (Auto)

A human being is a part of the whole, called by us Universe, a part limited in time and space. He experiences himself, his thoughts and feelings as something separated from the rest, a kind of optical delusion of his consciousness. This delusion is a kind of prison, restricting us to our personal desires and to affection for a few persons nearest to us. Our task must be to free from this prison by widening our circle of compassion to embrace all living creatures and the whole nature in its beauty.
Albert Einstein

7/9 point

Above: Leading has a great impact on the tonal color of text on a page. If, for instance, letter and word spacing appear too open, an increase in leading will help to even out the texture. Be sure you know what auto-leading means. It often has a default value of 120 per cent, i.e. 20 percent extra leading over and above the type size.

"auto," which usually has a value of 120 per cent of the type size. For 10 pt type, "auto" leading will thus produce baselines that are 12 pt apart (written 10/12, and pronounced "ten on twelve"). It is often said that most text faces need a few points of leading (note the old usage, meaning extra space between lines), and in average text settings "auto" leading will always produce readable text. Again, few jobs are average, and "auto" leading will often introduce too much space between lines, making the block of text look pale and uninteresting. You could as a habit to replace "auto" leading immediately with a definite value—start with leading equal to the type size ("set solid"), and then assess the effect of increasing the value in, say, 0.25 pt increments.

Leading may be applied to text locally as required, but that risks irregularities. Consistency is as vital to typographic spacing as to well-modulated speech. Text that hiccoughs along in unregulated bursts will distract the reader, diminishing the effectiveness of the message. There are several ways to control vertical spacing in an automated way.

PARAGRAPH SPACING

If you want paragraph spacing, you could just add a blank line (i.e. key two returns). But blank lines or multiple blank lines are not always appropriate. Using paragraph formatting allows you to specify any value as extra space between the paragraphs.

Humanity needs practical men, who get the most out of their work, and, without forgetting the general good, safeguard their own interests. But humanity also needs dreamers, for whom the disinterested development of an enterprise is so captivating that it becomes impossible for them to devote their care to their own material profit.

Without doubt, these dreamers do not deserve wealth, because they do not desire it. Even so, a well-organized society should assure to such workers the efficient means of accomplishing their task, in a life freed from material care and freely consecrated to research.

Marie Curie

1 mm Space After paragraph

Above: "Space After" is a useful way of controlling and editing paragraph spacing globally without having to key in extra returns to provide white space. If a "Space Before" value is also given, it will be added to any "Space After." "Space Before" is usually best kept for headings, where additional space is required to set it off further from the previous paragraph.

Humanity needs practical men, who get the most out of their work, and, without forgetting the general good, safeguard their own interests. But humanity also needs dreamers, for whom the disinterested development of an enterprise is so captivating that it becomes impossible for them to devote their care to their own material profit.

Without doubt, these dreamers do not deserve wealth, because they do not desire it. Even so, a well-organized society should assure to such workers the efficient means of accomplishing their task, in a life freed from material care and freely consecrated to research.

Marie Curie

1 line space after paragraph.

MANY PURISTS like the baselines of type in one column of text to align accurately with the baselines in neighbouring columns. This contributes greatly to the beauty of good text setting, but it is not always easy to accomplish.

The baseline grid

9

As headings, cross-headings, and paragraph spaces, all of different sizes, are introduced of into a run of text, the baselines in one column can soon get out of step with those in the next. This is where the baseline grid and the "snap to" feature comes in. Most software allows you to set a grid of equally spaced horizontal lines to which all your baselines can be snapped; you can specify how far down the page the grid starts, and how far apart the gridlines should be. If you apply "snap to grid" to your text, all the baselines will be forced to align with the grid, even if you have given different paragraphs different leading values. With grid increment and leading equal, you will see no response if you reduce the leading: the type is constrained to the grid. Equally, you will see too much response if you increase the leading: the type will snap to alternate gridlines.

To escape this straitjacket, you could apply "snap to grid" to some paragraphs and not others —but then why bother with a baseline grid at all? Why introduce irregularity to a grid that was meant to give regularity? It might be better to design our typographic detailing around the regularity of the incremental size of the baseline grid. If we decide that 10 pt text in our chosen type should have 11 pt leading, paragraphs could be 10/11, major headings could be 24/33, and

subheads 14/22, with space after paragraphs and extra space before headings also specified in 11 pt increments. With picture boxes also dimensioned in multiples of 11 point, it will be seen that the whole page structure, in vertical terms, would create satisfying horizontal stresses and be devoid of unsightly stepping from column to column. Grids should serve our needs; we are not slaves to the grid.

BASELINE SHIFT
Baseline shift is an extremely useful way of handling small vertical spacing problems. Despite its benefits, there are times when mathematical regularity is just not good enough, e.g. when a full line of capitals falls between two lines of upper- and lowercase letters, or when capitals are vertically centered in a text box.

STYLE SHEETS
Leading and paragraph spacing may be incorporated into a style sheet, along with all other aspects of control, including tracking, baseline shift, and H&Js. By using styles, you can ensure that all aspects of your setting, including both horizontal and vertical spacing, remain constant and consistent. Style sheets are probably the most effective and productive way of controlling our work.

Thomas Jefferson

To Jean Nicholas Demeunier, 1786

"What a stupendous, what an incomprehensible machine is man! Who can endure toil, famine, stripes, imprisonment & death itself in vindication of his own liberty, and the next moment inflict on his fellow men a bondage, one hour of which is fraught with more misery than ages of that which he rose in rebellion to oppose."

To Congress, 1806

"I agree with you that it is the duty of every good citizen to use all the opportunities, which occur to him, for preserving documents relating to the history of our country."

To John Wyche, 1809

"I have often thought that nothing would do more extensive good at small expense than the establishment of a small circulating library in every county, to consist of a few well-chosen books, to be lent to the people of the country under regulations as would secure their safe return in due time."

To Miles King, 1814

"Our particular principles of religion are a subject of accountability to our god alone. I enquire after no man's and trouble none with mine; nor is it given to us in this life to know whether yours or mine, our friend's or our foe's, are exactly the right."

Left: The major heading and the subheads, though different in size from the 7/9.5 point text, have leading values that are multiples of 9.5 pt and therefore sit exactly on the underlying baseline grid.

fellow men a bondage, one hour of which is fraught with more misery than ages of that which he rose in rebellion to oppose."

To Congress, 1806

"I agree with you that it is the duty of every good citizen to use all the opportunities, which occur to him, for preserving documents relating to the history of our country."

To John Wyche, 1809

"I have often thought that nothing would do more extensive good at small expense than the establishment of a small circulating library

Left: The subhead has a baseline shift of +2.0 pt, which raises it without altering the integrity of the baseline grid.

SEMIOTICS is the study of how meaning is created and communicated, and in particular by means of symbols and signs. In typographic design it can be applied to the selection of a particular typeface because it is suggestive of the meaning of a word or phrase to which it has been applied.

Semiotics

9

For the designer the choice of typeface can be bewildering. With tens of thousands to choose from the selection often falls to personal preference or the desire to use a new face that has become fashionable. This of course is not the way to do it

Legibility is of fundamental importance as a typeface is used to format words and the purpose of words is to communicate their meaning. For example a closely packed directory that uses very small text needs a type that is designed for the job, like "Unit" or "Meta," whereas for an up

market real estate prospectus, a finely chiseled Old Style serif might be more appropriate.

But beyond legibility is another factor, whether or not a typeface is stylistically appropriate for the job in hand, and this is where semiotics comes in. This applies primarily to display size type. As the examples opposite demonstrate, many typefaces have strong associations sometimes because of their inherent design or because of their past usage. A typeface like the aptly named "Playbill" is for ever associated with popular entertainment and the Old West.

Left: In the best of all circumstances the choice of font will be appropriate stylistically as well as from the legibility standpoint. Here "Optima" works perfectly for this arts program.

FEAR Onyx

Cake

Cooper Black

Journal

Versa Pro Italic

Relax

EnglSchreibschrift

WANTED

Playbill

SCIENCE

Bank Gothic

RUGGED Square Slab Serif

Centaur CALM

WIN Franklin Gothic Heavy Italic

Many typefaces evoke a mood or project an emotion. A few words set in some familar typefaces demonstrates the point.

IN THE DAYS BEFORE page-layout applications came within everyone's reach, typesetters, who had learned and practiced their trade in the printing world, knew the difference between en (–) and em (—) dashes, typographer's quote marks ("), inch or tick (") marks, and so on. The designer needs to know when and how to use them.

Typographic conventions

WORD SPACES AND TABS

The rule to remember is that there must only ever be one space between any two words. This means that you should never find two word spaces or two tab "spaces" in a row.

The idea of using two spaces is a hangover from the days of typewriters when people, restricted by a typewriter's single monospaced typeface, used two spaces to emphasize the end of a sentence and multiple tabs to line up text. Proportional-width fonts, however, are not "fixed" in the same way; each character sits the width it needs and no more, so you don't need to override anything. If you use multiple tab spaces to line up text, and then change fonts, applications, or even change printers, you'll find your tabulation goes out of alignment. Keep the rule in mind: use one tab space only and then manually set your tabs in the correct places on the formatting ruler to achieve the effect you want.

CURLY AND STRAIGHT QUOTATION MARKS

The rules for quotation marks are:

Straight single and double quotation marks are used to denote feet and inches respectively; curly quotation marks should be used for all "quotation" purposes

Double quotation marks are all you need for quoted speech, quotations, and to indicate slang, idioms, or vernacular words. (However single quotation marks are more often used for this purpose in text aimed at the UK.)

Some people use single quotation marks within double to define a quotation inside another quotation, or the other way around (i.e. double quotation marks within single), but this is for reasons of clarity only

Many programs have an option for Smart Quotes, which will automatically insert the correctly facing curly quotation marks. If you have to import text with straight quotation marks from a text file, remember to check the Convert Quotes box first.

You might strike a problem with your software if you need to insert an apostrophe at the start of a word, for example:

'twas the night before Christmas

Smart Quotes will automatically insert an opening quotation mark rather than an apostrophe. You can fool your computer into thinking it needs to use an apostrophe by first typing:

x'twas the night before Christmas

Then removing the x.

DASHES AND HYPHENS

Hyphens are used only to hyphenate a pair of words, such as "export-strength," or to link two parts of a word broken at the end of a line. For all other purposes, a dash is required. Dashes are of two types: en dashes (–) and em dashes (—). Em dashes are twice as wide as en dashes, being based on the widths of the letters "n" and "m" respectively.

U.S./UK USAGE DIFFERENCES

The main uses for em dashes in text aimed at the American market is to surround a parenthetical phrase—such as this one—and they are used without spaces on either side. (In text aimed at the UK, en dashes are used for this, with spaces before and after.) Em dashes are also commonly used in tables (to indicate the absence of data, or repeated data, e.g., in bibliographies) and to introduce lines of dialog. Em dashes are also used to indicate when speech is interrupted.

En dashes are used in text in both the United States and the UK to take the place of words such as "to" and "from" between dates, for example in "the 1939–45 war," or in pairs of words such as "input–output."

ELLIPSES

To indicate missing words, the correct typographical mark to use is an ellipsis: this consists of three dots and should have a character space before and after (or, at the end of a sentence, a period immediately after). Don't use three periods: you will find a "proper" ellipsis in the character set of any font.

HANGING PUNCTUATION

Punctuation characters normally fall inside the column width of set text. When they are at the start or end of a line, they can sometimes create the appearance of ugly indents in the text and disrupt an otherwise uniform margin.

In extensive amounts of relatively small running text, these indents will not be so apparent. But when small amounts of text form a visual focal point, steps need to be taken to correct problems caused by end-of-line punctuation. InDesign has an automatic hanging punctuation feature called "optical margins." Most punctuation characters that appear at the start or end of a line, such as start quotes, end quotes, hyphens, full points, and commas, will be pushed away from the flush edge of type. Colons and semicolons, in view of their shape, are not hung.

" Democracy means simply the bludgeoning of the people by the people for the people."

" Experience is the name that everyone gives to their mistakes."

" Fashion is a form of ugliness so intolerable that we have to alter it every six months."

" For those who like that sort of thing, it's the sort of thing that they like."

" I hope you have not been leading a double life, pretending to be wicked and being really good all the time. That would be hypocrisy."

" I sometimes think that God, in creating man, overestimated His ability."

Oscar Wilde

Above: Hanging punctuation can be created easily using InDesign's optical margin feature.

FONT IDENTIFIER

FREEFORM

SCRIPT

DISPLAY

SANS-SERIF

SERIF

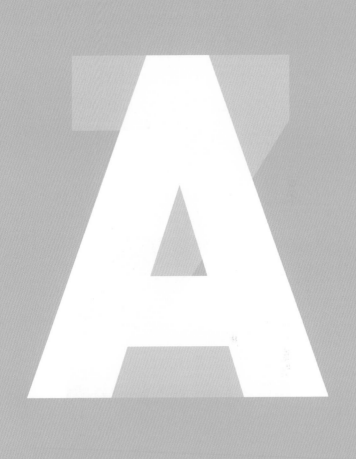

Angie

As much a "stressed sans" as it is a serif design, Angie is a font family with serifs that are little more than hints. It is impressively legible at small sizes, but the subtleties of the character shapes require high-quality printing to render accurately.

ABCDEFGHIJKLM
NOPQRSTUVWXYZ
abcdefghijklm
nopqrstuvwxyz
1234567890@&!?;:"*

Angkoon

Angkoon is a typeface family with an exceptionally large number of variants—four weights, with italics and small-cap options, too. It has an obvious calligraphic base, but it has a restrained clarity that makes it useful for many other text-setting purposes.

ABCDEFGHIJKLM
NOPQRSTUVWXYZ
abcdefghijklm
nopqrstuvwxyz
1234567890@&!?;:"*

Arepo

Sumner Stone's Arepo is a decorative face created to accompany a number of other of his typefaces, including Stone Print and Cycles. The relatively narrow characters and extreme thins show a distinct elegance, especially in the Italic and Italic Swash variants.

ABCDEFGHIJKLM
NOPQRSTUVWXYZ
abcdefghijklm
nopqrstuvwxyz
1234567890@&!?;:"*

Atma

For a serif family that's good for book typesetting and provides a wide range of weights and options, Atma's 96-strong set is hard to beat. It has strong Transitional characteristics and was crafted for exceptional legibility at small sizes.

ABCDEFGHIJKLM
NOPQRSTUVWXYZ
abcdefghijklm
nopqrstuvwxyz
1234567890@&!?;:"*

Baskerville

Designed in 1706 by John Baskerville, this font represented a milestone in typographic development that took advantage of the latest printing developments. At the time, some claimed that the contrasting thick and thin elements would damage eyesight, but it has long been recognized as a very usable classic.

ABCDEFGHIJKLM
NOPQRSTUVWXYZ
abcdefghijklm
nopqrstuvwxyz
1234567890@&!?;:"*

Bodoni

This version of Bauer Bodoni came from the Bauersche Giesserei foundry in the 1920s. It is a careful and precise revival of the face created by Giambattista Bodoni in the late 18th century, and is distinguished by crisp, fine serifs and extreme weight differences between the thick and thin strokes.

ABCDEFGHIJKLM
NOPQRSTUVWXYZ
abcdefghijklm
nopqrstuvwxyz
1234567890@&!?;:"*

B

Belwe

A font influenced by Art Nouveau design ideas as well as older blackletter styles. It has shapes and angles that vary throughout the different characters, yet it all works together as a coherent whole. It was designed by Georg Belwe in 1926 for a type foundry in Dresden, Germany.

ABCDEFGHIJKLM
NOPQRSTUVWXYZ
abcdefghijklm
nopqrstuvwxyz
1234567890@&!?;:"'*

Bembo

The origins of Bembo lie in a face first printed in 1495 by Aldus Manutius. While it was incredibly influential in typeface design, it was Stanley Morison's 1929 project for Monotype that produced the Bembo we know today—slightly rationalized and with a reformed italic. A classic design suitable for a wide variety of uses.

ABCDEFGHIJKLM
NOPQRSTUVWXYZ
abcdefghijklm
nopqrstuvwxyz
1234567890@&!?;:"'★

Brioso

Named after the Italian word for "lively," the Brioso family is an unashamedly calligraphic design crafted as a well-balanced and extensive family of body text-friendly faces. This can instill the impression of a traditional hand-lettered manuscript without straying too far from proper typesetting control.

ABCDEFGHIJKLM
NOPQRSTUVWXYZ
abcdefghijklm
nopqrstuvwxyz
1234567890@&!?;:"'*

Caecilia

A subtly sophisticated design suitable for a very wide range of uses. Although it appears at a glance to be a monoline, slab-serifed face, it has subtle stroke variations, a delicate open design, and an almost exuberant set of italics.

ABCDEFGHIJKLM
NOPQRSTUVWXYZ
abcdefghijklm
nopqrstuvwxyz
1234567890@&!?;:"*

Caslon 3

William Caslon's eponymous typeface was known as the "script of kings"—and republicans as well, as it was also used in the American Declaration of Independence. This influential design is regarded as being as reliable today as it was in the 18th century.

ABCDEFGHIJKLM
NOPQRSTUVWXYZ
abcdefghijklm
nopqrstuvwxyz
1234567890@&!?;:"*

Cellini

A fine example of a Didone type design, although it was created by Albert Boton in 2003 rather than in the 18th century. It is available in Titling cuts with very fine thin strokes as well as the regular forms that are more suitable for body text.

ABCDEFGHIJKLM
NOPQRSTUVWXYZ
abcdefghijklm
nopqrstuvwxyz
1234567890@&!?;:"*

C

Centaur

It began as a face made for the Metropolitan Museum in 1914, and was based on Nicolas Jenson's Renaissance printing. Curiously, the italic came later and from a different source, but they work together as a harmonious, elegant Venetian font suitable for body text and for headlines.

ABCDEFGHIJKLM
NOPQRSTUVWXYZ
abcdefghijklm
nopqrstuvwxyz
1234567890@&!?;:"✲

Century

This font appeared in 1894 and is a good example of the typographic Neo-Renaissance of the period. It was created for use in Century Magazine as a more solid and readable design than previous fonts, but it has since been remade many times in subtly different forms.

ABCDEFGHIJKLM
NOPQRSTUVWXYZ
abcdefghijklm
nopqrstuvwxyz
1234567890@&!?;:"*

Chaparral

It's character combines a strong, highly legible slab-serif design with the graceful style of book lettering from centuries earlier to deliver an extensive, coherent typeface family with the flexibility to be used almost anywhere, from small text to demanding display use.

ABCDEFGHIJKLM
NOPQRSTUVWXYZ
abcdefghijklm
nopqrstuvwxyz
1234567890@&!?;:"*

Cheltenham

Created at the beginning of the 20th century, the gently idiosyncratic Cheltenham was intended more for "ephemeral" print use than for extended passages of text. The modern cuts finished in the 1970s have a slightly larger x-height than the original and suit a wider range of purposes.

ABCDEFGHIJKLM
NOPQRSTUVWXYZ
abcdefghijklm
nopqrstuvwxyz
1234567890@&!?;:"*

Cicero

Cicero is best described as a semi-serif design, dispensing with most serifs other than those that would occur naturally if drawing the letters with a flat-nib pen. This gives it a modern clarity and allows for particularly tight setting while retaining certain basic serif qualities.

ABCDEFGHIJKLM
NOPQRSTUVWXYZ
abcdefghijklm
nopqrstuvwxyz
1234567890@&!?;:"*

City

The slab-serif Berthold City was designed by Georg Trump in 1930. It has unusually square characteristics, with counters in the letterforms having pure right angles and outer lines neatly rounded at the corners. It works well for short passages of text as well as advertising and display.

ABCDEFGHIJKLM
NOPQRSTUVWXYZ
abcdefghijklm
nopqrstuvwxyz
1234567890@&!?;:"*

C

Clarendon

Originating in the mid-19th century, and named for the Clarendon Press in Oxford, the slab-serifed Clarendon was created to work with standard, lighter serif faces. The typeface was revived a little over 100 years later, and is often used in headlines. It has certain basic serif qualities.

ABCDEFGHIJKLM
NOPQRSTUVWXYZ
abcdefghijklm
nopqrstuvwxyz
1234567890&!?;:"*

Cochin

Although copper engravings from the 18th century were the basis for Georges Peignot's Cochin, it shows an unusual mix of styles. The result is elegant and effective, and was particularly popular in the early 20th century when it was created.

ABCDEFGHIJKLM
NOPQRSTUVWXYZ
abcdefghijklm
nopqrstuvwxyz
1234567890@&!?;:"*

Cooper

The strong, rounded forms of Cooper Black are a familiar sight in signage and advertising. Made in 1922 by Oswald Cooper, an American advertising and type designer, the family was extended to include italics and different weights. Surprisingly useful, especially in lighter weights.

ABCDEFGHIJKLM
NOPQRSTUVWXYZ
abcdefghijklm
nopqrstuvwxyz
1234567890&!?;:"*

Craw modern

A Didone design with Victorian-era poster font qualities, Craw Modern, by Freeman Craw, is a strong, wide-set typeface with self-assured characteristics. The italics have bold flourishes, and the bold in particular has impressive extremes in stroke weights. Used in headline and other display type situations.

ABCDEFGHIJKLM
NOPQRSTUVWXYZ
abcdefghijklm
nopqrstuvwxyz
1234567890@&!?;:"*

Danubia

This is a Didone-style typeface family with a sharply vertical stress to heavy strokes and simple but strong serifs. Although it was designed in 2002 it has a strong early 20th-century period feeling, particularly if mixed (carefully) with its sibling font, Danuvia Script.

ABCDEFGHIJKLM
NOPQRSTUVWXYZ
abcdefghijklm
nopqrstuvwxyz
1234567890@&!?;:"*

Delphin

Designed in the 1950s by George Trump, the lowercase characters of this font have a handwritten flourish that contrasts very interestingly with the more traditional capitals. Formal yet casual in feel, Delphin works well in shorter literary settings, for example lyrics and poems.

ABCDEFGHIJKLM
NOPQRSTUVWXYZ
abcdefghijklm
nopqrstuvwxyz
1234567890@&!?;:"*

Democratica

Created Miles Newlyn, a graduate of Central Saint Martin's in London, Democratica is a deconstructivist typeface design that appears to be built up ingeniously out of type fragments into a coherent, albeit highly distinctive, font. Note how the capitals are the same height as the lowercase body. Useful in short bursts.

ABCDEFGHIJKLM
NOPQRSTUVWXYZ
abcdefghijklm
nopqrstuvwxyz
1234567890@&!?;:'"*

Didot

Originating in the type designs of Firmin Didot it is an often-copied design from the Enlightenment period, and it has a highly classical, elegant feel. The vertical stresses, unbracketed serifs, and extremes of stroke weight are all distinctive characteristics.

ABCDEFGHIJKLM
NOPQRSTUVWXYZ
abcdefghijklm
nopqrstuvwxyz
1234567890@&!?;:"*

Dyadis

Names for the Latin for "duality," this font is an intriguing mix of serif and sans-serif forms derived from fonts dating from the 1920s and 1930s. The design manages to combine a sparse elegance with clarity and a distinctive individuality.

ABCDEFGHIJKLM
NOPQRSTUVWXYZ
abcdefghijklm
nopqrstuvwxyz
1234567890@&!?;:"*

Egyptienne

Adian Frutiger's Egyptienne was made in 1956, and it was the first face designed specifically for photosetting and litho printing. The large x-height and clear forms help it work well across a wide range of uses. Not to be confused with Egyptienne family from URW++ .

ABCDEFGHIJKLM
NOPQRSTUVWXYZ
abcdefghijklm
nopqrstuvwxyz
1234567890@&!?;:"*

E

Electra

This font was designed in 1935 by William Dwiggins, and this distinctive Transitional family has remained popular for book use ever since. It is equally useful for display work, where its bright, pen-derived features give text an urgent, lively quality.

ABCDEFGHIJKLM
NOPQRSTUVWXYZ
abcdefghijklm
nopqrstuvwxyz
1234567890@&!?;:"*

Elysa

Hans Edward Meier's Elysa is a restrained yet clearly pen-derived calligraphic font with an extra-ordinarily large family. It includes weights from light to bold, with multiple swash variants, regular and old-style numerals, small caps, and even calligraphic ornaments.

ABCDEFGHIJKLM
NOPQRSTUVWXYZ
abcdefghijklm
nopqrstuvwxyz
1234567890@&!?;:"*

Enigma

Designed by Jeremy Tankard, Enigma is a rather beautiful, traditionally constructed font. It is an upright Transitional design with crisply cut modern touches that balance the underlying script-influenced rotunda form. The result is legible at small book-text sizes, yet strong and individual in advertising and display contexts.

ABCDEFGHIJKLM
NOPQRSTUVWXYZ
abcdefghijklm
nopqrstuvwxyz
1234567890@&!?;:"*

Eureka

Created in 2002, this serif typeface is part of a large family that includes sans, mono, and "antique" forms. Eureka is designed along the lines of a classic letterpress font, with relatively little difference in stroke width and clean serifs. The italics in particular have a spartan elegance.

ABCDEFGHIJKLM
NOPQRSTUVWXYZ
abcdefghijklm
nopqrstuvwxyz
1234567890@&!?;:"*

Excalibur

A product of the Elsner & Flake type design foundry, Excalibur is a highly condensed design that is largely Transitional in style. This comes in just two weights and no styles, and it best reserved for headlines and other display-style uses.

ABCDEFGHIJKLM
NOPQRSTUVWXYZ
abcdefghijklm
nopqrstuvwxyz
1234567890&!?;:"*

Fairbank

One story claims that this 1929 design was created as an italic companion for Bembo, but the designer, the influential Alfred Fairbank, says it was drawn independently. It was discovered and expanded in recent years as a digital revival, and provides the user with a distinguished Italianate grace.

ABCDEFGHIJKLM
NOPQRSTUVWXYZ
abcdefghijklm
nopqrstuvwxyz
1234567890@ﬅ!?;:"ʻ

Fairfield

Based on 15th- and 16th-century Venetian fonts, although with more than a hint of later Didone upright precision, Fairfield was made to be clear and legible at body-text sizes. The italic forms are only slightly slanted, with swash faces providing the face's more distinctive curves.

ABCDEFGHIJKLM
NOPQRSTUVWXYZ
abcdefghijklm
nopqrstuvwxyz
1234567890@&!?;:"*

Fedra

A cunning mix of humanist form and mathematical construction, Fedra Serif is part of a broad type family. Fedra Serif A's proportions match Fedra Sans, while Fedra Serif B has longer stems and more weight difference between strokes. All character widths and metrics match to make them smoothly interchangeable.

ABCDEFGHIJKLM
NOPQRSTUVWXYZ
abcdefghijklm
nopqrstuvwxyz
1234567890@&!?;:"*

Fenice

Created in 1980 by Aldo Novarese, Fenice has serifs that are strongly influenced by Didone faces such as Bodoni, but uses them in a less mathematically purist letterform. It sets fairly compactly, and so uses space on the page efficiently. Fenice is pronounced "fe-nee-chay."

ABCDEFGHIJKLM
NOPQRSTUVWXYZ
abcdefghijklm
nopqrstuvwxyz
1234567890@&!?;:"*

Fournier

Designed in the mid-18th century by Pierre Simon Fournier and revived by Monotype in 1924, this represents the beginnings of the Transitional era of type design. The stress is more vertical and stroke weight contrast is greater than earlier type. This gives a light, even look to book typography.

ABCDEFGHIJKLM
NOPQRSTUVWXYZ
abcdefghijklm
nopqrstuvwxyz
1234567890&!?;:"*

Fresco

Created by the well-known Fred Smeijers, Fresco is a highly legible, simple serif design intended mainly for small-text use. It has very little variation in stroke width—in the lighter weights it is practically a monoline—and the serifs are essentially simple stroke continuations and caps.

ABCDEFGHIJKLM
NOPQRSTUVWXYZ
abcdefghijklm
nopqrstuvwxyz
1234567890@&!?;:"*

Garamond

Claude Garamond's eponymous 16th-century typeface has probably been recut and redrawn more than any other font in history. Curiously, many Garamonds are actually based on 17th-century Garamond interpretations by Jean Jannon. Some are delicate, others more lively, but all share an impressive elegance and sophistication.

ABCDEFGHIJKLM
NOPQRSTUVWXYZ
abcdefghijklm
nopqrstuvwxyz
1234567890@&!?;:"'*

G

Glypha

Created by Adrian Frutiger, Glypha is a slab-serif design that is based on his earlier Serifa design, but with a larger x-height for more general legibility in varying circumstances. It uses the same general number-based design scheme as the popular Univers family.

ABCDEFGHIJKLM
NOPQRSTUVWXYZ
abcdefghijklm
nopqrstuvwxyz
1234567890&!?;:"*

Golden Cockerel

This elegant font is based on designs by Eric Gill for the Gold Cockerel Press. Gill's skills in stone carving, wood engraving, and calligraphy all contributed to this graceful typeface family. The family includes titling and initials and ornaments as well as roman and italics for book printing.

ABCDEFGHIJKLM
NOPQRSTUVWXYZ
abcdefghijklm
nopqrstuvwxyz
1234567890&!?;:"*

Goudy

It is often said to be the most popular typeface ever made, and appears regularly in packaging and display advertising. Created by Frederic Goudy in 1915 and expanded through the next decade, this family is packed with Goudy's unique detailing. A display standard that should always be on hand.

G

ABCDEFGHIJKLM
NOPQRSTUVWXYZ
abcdefghijklm
nopqrstuvwxyz
1234567890&!?;:"*

Grantofte

A serif display face derived from the wooden carved lettering found on old sailing ships, Grantofte has a simple, slightly old-fashioned feel that sets very well in headlines and short passages. This comes in just Regular and Bold weights, plus an italic with swash-style capitals.

ABCDEFGHIJKLM
NOPQRSTUVWXYZ
abcdefghijklm
nopqrstuvwxyz
1234567890@&!?;:"*

Haverj

Based on lettering drawn in the 1970s, this design is a serif face that works well in text and display setting, but note the subtle quirks in the stroke terminals and serifs that give it a slight eccentricity. Haverj is an Armenian girls' name meaning "forever" or "eternally."

ABCDEFGHIJKLM
NOPQRSTUVWXYZ
abcdefghijklm
nopqrstuvwxyz
1234567890@&!?;:"*

Humana Serif

This font balances humanistic and slightly flamboyant character shapes with a crisp precision of form. This is a little too lively for paragraph-level type, but it is an exceptionally good casual display face. Not to be confused with the rather Italianate version of Humana from Linotype.

ABCDEFGHIJKLM
NOPQRSTUVWXYZ
abcdefghijklm
nopqrstuvwxyz
1234567890@&!?;:"*

Industrial

A rather elegant Didone-style face from 1908, produced in Turin. More condensed than many of this style, it has surprisingly bold geometric serifs on some of the capitals. This sets very bright, and the italic face almost sparkles on the page. Superb for making a headline statement.

ABCDEFGHIJKLM
NOPQRSTUVWXYZ
abcdefghijklm
nopqrstuvwxyz
1234567890@&!?;:"*

Ionic

This first appeared as an essentially Egyptian display face cut in 1821, but it was refined 40 years later to have a stronger stroke contrast and bracketed serifs. Ionic became a popular choice in the newspaper industry, and helped set the standard for later newspaper designs.

ABCDEFGHIJKLM
NOPQRSTUVWXYZ
abcdefghijklm
nopqrstuvwxyz
1234567890&!?;:"*

Italia

This is a font, based on Golden Type, with slightly rounded slab serifs. The most obvious feature, however, is the slanted upper serifs on most of the lowercase characters. Use for display setting and in short texts where these features are a benefit.

ABCDEFGHIJKLM
NOPQRSTUVWXYZ
abcdefghijklm
nopqrstuvwxyz
1234567890@&!?;:"*

Janson

Originally cut by Hungarian monk Miklós Kis in 1690 and named after Dutch printer Anton Janson (not Nicolas Jenson), this typeface has strong but not heavy forms, with a good contrast between stroke weights. It has remained popular for book and magazine use since its introduction.

ABCDEFGHIJKLM
NOPQRSTUVWXYZ
abcdefghijklm
nopqrstuvwxyz
1234567890@&!?;:"*

Jenson

Adobe's Jenson Pro is a careful revival of Nicolas Jenson's influential Renassance fonts, but with a modern regularity and precision that makes it exceptionally broadly usable. This lends an air of traditional refinement to body text and, when used appropriately, to headlines and display work as well.

ABCDEFGHIJKLM
NOPQRSTUVWXYZ
abcdefghijklm
nopqrstuvwxyz
1234567890@&!?;:"*

Joanna

This was drawn by Eric Gill for his personal use in his hand-run Joanna Press work, and meant as a continuation of William Morris's Arts and Crafts aesthetics and ideals. It has unusually condensed and practically upright italics, and its austere beauty combines particularly well with Gill Sans.

ABCDEFGHIJKLM
NOPQRSTUVWXYZ
abcdefghijklm
nopqrstuvwxyz
1234567890@&!?;:'"*

Kallos

A clearly pen-based calligraphic design, this has a distinct flair but manages to remain usable for body text use as well as display work. Note the long ascenders and descenders that help give it a feel of hand-lettered elegance.

ABCDEFGHIJKLM
NOPQRSTUVWXYZ
abcdefghijklm
nopqrstuvwxyz
1234567890@&!?;:'"*

Kiev

A calligraphic-influenced font design created by Viktor Kharyk and named after the capital of Ukraine. Key characteristics of this lively design are the jaunty shapes and the use of open counters and disconnected strokes. Despite the relatively heavy lines, this gives it a crisp and light feel.

ABCDEFGHIJKLM
NOPQRSTUVWXYZ
abcdefghijklm
nopqrstuvwxyz
1234567890@ &!?;:'"*

Laricio

Named after the Italian term for the Larch tree, Laricio introduces a slightly organic touch to otherwise traditional letterforms. There is a slight tendency for serifs to fly to the left, but apart from this the serifs in the capital letterforms are relatively minimal.

ABCDEFGHIJKLM
NOPQRSTUVWXYZ
abcdefghijklm
nopqrstuvwxyz
1234567890@&!?;:"*

Literaturnaya

One of the most popular serif fonts in Soviet printing, this largely Venetian face was designed around 1940 and was based on Berthold's Latinskaya, the Cyrillic version of Lateinische, from 40 years earlier. A fair choice for traditional text setting, and of course provides a complete Cyrillic character set.

ABCDEFGHIJKLM
NOPQRSTUVWXYZ
abcdefghijklm
nopqrstuvwxyz
1234567890@&!?;:"*

Lubalin Graph

A strongly geometric face based on Herb Lubalin's Avant Garde, this is a monoline Egyptian design with a sturdy, open look and a large x-height. An excellent choice for conveying a no-nonsense quality in display and advertising work, but not normally suitable for small text use.

ABCDEFGHIJKLM
NOPQRSTUVWXYZ
abcdefghijklm
nopqrstuvwxyz
1234567890@&!?;:"*

FONT IDENTIFIER

Lucida

Part of an extraordinarily large design range including Lucida Calligraphy, Casual, Fax, Blackletter, Sans, and more, and with qualities that help it remain legible even in low-resolution print and display, this is a good choice for all forms of typesetting where a quietly modern feel is desired.

ABCDEFGHIJKLM
NOPQRSTUVWXYZ
abcdefghijklm
nopqrstuvwxyz
1234567890@&!?;:"*

Melior

A creation of the prolific Hermann Zapf, Melior is a robust, open design with a slightly square form that gives it a stately feel. Use this family with confidence in anything from fine book typography to big display work.

ABCDEFGHIJKLM
NOPQRSTUVWXYZ
abcdefghijklm
nopqrstuvwxyz
1234567890@&!?;:"*

Memphis

The slab-serif Egyptian design of Memphis combines with a highly geometric form, giving it a neutral, rational clarity. This was the first revival of the Egyptian form, and was made by Rudolf Wolf in 1929. Use primarily in advertising, packaging, and display work.

ABCDEFGHIJKLM
NOPQRSTUVWXYZ
abcdefghijklm
nopqrstuvwxyz
1234567890@&!?;:"*

Minion

A 1990 design by Robert Slimbach, Minion was modeled on typefaces from the late Renaissance. It has the elegance of type from this period, but it has a family range of extraordinary breadth. Created initially as a book font, Minion has been used across a great many kinds of work.

ABCDEFGHIJKLM
NOPQRSTUVWXYZ
abcdefghijklm
nopqrstuvwxyz
1234567890@&!?;:"*

Mirarae

Carol Twombly's Mirarae is a broad, open design with italic calligraphic influences; the two weights are a kind of cross between upright and cursive forms. This won an international type design competition when it debuted in 1984.

ABCDEFGHIJKLM
NOPQRSTUVWXYZ
abcdefghijklm
nopqrstuvwxyz
1234567890@&!?;:"*

Monteverdi

Monteverdi's steadfast capitals are teamed with a diminutive but carefully balanced lowercase. The designer Lars Bergquist gave this family some absolutely beautiful touches, and the flourishes in the italic are exquisite. Better suited to larger type because of the small x-height, although it remains clear at small sizes.

ABCDEFGHIJKLM
NOPQRSTUVWXYZ
abcdefghijklm
nopqrstuvwxyz
1234567890@&!?;:"*

Mrs Eaves

Named after John Baskerville's housekeeper, who later became his wife, Mrs Eaves is a Transitional design with a huge range of alternates, small caps, ligatures, and other typographic gems. The upright faces set more widely than most fonts, but is an effective choice for fine book typography.

ABCDEFGHIJKLM
NOPQRSTUVWXYZ
abcdefghijklm
nopqrstuvwxyz
1234567890@&!?;:"*

Napoleone Slab

This is a slab-serif design with a difference; it has true italics, old-style numerals, and even ligatures. However, it is also a geometric-influenced face with angles and curves that work well in faxes and on screens and for setting panels of information.

ABCDEFGHIJKLM
NOPQRSTUVWXYZ
abcdefghijklm
nopqrstuvwxyz
1234567890@&!?;:"*

Obelisk

Phill Grimshaw's striking Obelisk uses chiseled, cut strokes rather than pen-drawn ones. The letterforms show an occasional dashing disregard for sticking to the baseline, giving it a distinctly lively character. The lighter weights can work for short passages at medium sizes, while the bold makes for punchy headlines.

ABCDEFGHIJKLM
NOPQRSTUVWXYZ
abcdefghijklm
nopqrstuvwxyz
1234567890@&!?;:"*

O

Officina

Officina was created in 1990 by Eric Spiekermann and Just van Rossum as a traditional typographic take on office-based typewriter output. The regular widths and simple shapes keep it legible at small sizes and in crude output such as faxes. Try using it with the related Officina Sans.

ABCDEFGHIJKLM
NOPQRSTUVWXYZ
abcdefghijklm
nopqrstuvwxyz
1234567890@&!?;:"*

Oldrichium

This design has the core forms of classic book type but also the almost casual line qualities obtained through using a calligrapher's pen at high speed. Used small, the kinks can look like poor printing. But when set large enough for individual shapes to stand out, the effect is dramatic.

ABCDEFGHIJKLM
NOPQRSTUVWXYZ
abcdefghijklm
nopqrstuvwxyz
1234567890@&!?;:"*

Origami

At first glance, Origami would appear to be made from a succession of angles, but if you look more closely you'll see it is nothing but curves. It resulted from designs for a low-resolution typeface, and includes a Chancery-rooted italic. Use in small doses for maximum effect.

ABCDEFGHIJKLM
NOPQRSTUVWXYZ
abcdefghijklm
nopqrstuvwxyz
1234567890@&!?;:"*

Page Serif

The serifs in Page Serif give it a firm stability, and the strong, barely varying strokes help it remain legible at small sizes. This is an unfussy, almost utilitarian face, but one with enough style to perform well in many different situations.

ABCDEFGHIJKLM
NOPQRSTUVWXYZ
abcdefghijklm
nopqrstuvwxyz
1234567890@&!?;:"*

Palatino

A well-known Old Face design with calligraphic undertones, Palatino was created by Hermann Zapf during the late 1950s. One key goal was for it to remain legible even on crude paper. The typeface is named after Giambattista Palatino, a calligrapher from the early 16th century.

ABCDEFGHIJKLM
NOPQRSTUVWXYZ
abcdefghijklm
nopqrstuvwxyz
1234567890@&!?;:"*

Panther

Elsner & Flake's Panther is a curious typeface. The essentially Venetian or Garalde-based design is very slightly slanted and comes in just Regular and Bold versions, but it includes a few subtle quirks. The tail of the capital Q, for example, has an attractive, swash-like form.

ABCDEFGHIJKLM
NOPQRSTUVWXYZ
abcdefghijklm
nopqrstuvwxyz
1234567890@&!?;:"*

Perpetua

Perpetua was based on lettering found in old engravings and is Eric Gill's most popular serif design. The clean-cut lines give Perpetua-set text a quietly formal air, but the design is also full of touches that help it sparkle on the page. Curiously, the italic design was originally called Felicity.

ABCDEFGHIJKLM
NOPQRSTUVWXYZ
abcdefghijklm
nopqrstuvwxyz
1234567890&!?;:"*

Phaistos

This design from 1989–1991 by David Berlow is something of a revival of Rudolf Koch's 1922 Locarnon. The calligraphic formshave curiously tapered verticals and an almost cut quality to many of the curves. Use with care when a semi-formal, early 20th-century period feel is desired.

ABCDEFGHIJKLM
NOPQRSTUVWXYZ
abcdefghijklm
nopqrstuvwxyz
1234567890@&!?;:"*

Plantin

Plantin was made for Monotype in 1913 and named after 16th-century Dutch printer Christopher Plantin, although it isn't based on his work. The strong forms, large x-height, and subtly condensed shapes make it popular for books and journals, and the bolder designs work well in display setting.

ABCDEFGHIJKLM
NOPQRSTUVWXYZ
abcdefghijklm
nopqrstuvwxyz
1234567890@&!?;:"*

Prensa

This font, named after the Spanish word for "press," has a curious tension throughout the forms that give it a pronounced liveliness on the page; curves swell and shrink, and joins are delicate and sharp. Use primarily in display and advertising text rather than book setting.

ABCDEFGHIJKLM
NOPQRSTUVWXYZ
abcdefghijklm
nopqrstuvwxyz
1234567890@&!?;:"*

Quadraat

Quadraat is a trifle quirky, particularly in the heavier weights, but it remains a highly usable typeface, especially for display and advertising work. It is Venetian or Early Transitional at its core, but with subtle touches that betray its modern origins. The italics show almost brush-based characteristics.

ABCDEFGHIJKLM
NOPQRSTUVWXYZ
abcdefghijklm
nopqrstuvwxyz
1234567890@&!?;:"*

Reminga

A clear, reliable book face with delicate calligraphic touches that set it apart from the crowd. Note, for example, the slight angle of the horizontal bar in the capital A, the organic joint in the y, and so on. The titling faces are intended for larger use.

ABCDEFGHIJKLM
NOPQRSTUVWXYZ
abcdefghijklm
nopqrstuvwxyz
1234567890@&!?;:"*

R

Rockwell

A popular slab-serif face with an unvarying stroke width and a heavier than average appearance. Rockwell is superb for display work where a robust, mechanical feel is needed. The wide range of weights give it flexibility, from the sentence-friendly Rockwell Light to the attention-grabbing Extra Bold.

ABCDEFGHIJKLM
NOPQRSTUVWXYZ
abcdefghijklm
nopqrstuvwxyz
1234567890@&!?;:'"*

Romana

Romana originated as a French revival of Old Style type designs during the mid-19th century, first as a set of titling capitals and later as a complete typeface. It was immensely popular and was quickly copied around the world, being named Elzevier, Roemisch, Romanish, or Romaans in different countries.

ABCDEFGHIJKLM
NOPQRSTUVWXYZ
abcdefghijklm
nopqrstuvwxyz
1234567890@&!?;:"*

Rotis

Designed by Otl Aicher and named after the Bavarian village where he lives, Rotis was intended as a "font for all occasions." It comes in Serif, Semi Serif, Semi Sans, and Sans Serif forms, and it does, in fact, suit everything from book and magazines to posters and display text.

ABCDEFGHIJKLM
NOPQRSTUVWXYZ
abcdefghijklm
nopqrstuvwxyz
1234567890@&!?;:"*

Sabon

Designed by master typographer Jan Tschichold and released in 1967, Sabon's design roots lie in work by Claude Garamond and, for the italics, Robert Granjon. The goal was to produce a face that would work identically across multiple typesetting technologies. The result is an elegant and flexible face for text.

ABCDEFGHIJKLM
NOPQRSTUVWXYZ
abcdefghijklm
nopqrstuvwxyz
1234567890@&!?;:"*

Scala

A hybrid Transitional/Egyptian slab-serif face with sparse beauty and poise, the minimal variance in stroke width gives Scala clarity at small sizes as well as strength in display work. Note the availability of Scala Sans and Scala Jewels, a decorative titling set of faces.

ABCDEFGHIJKLM
NOPQRSTUVWXYZ
abcdefghijklm
nopqrstuvwxyz
1234567890@&!?;:"*

Scotch Roman

This is a good example of work from Scottish typographers, with wide proportions, extreme differences in stroke width, heavily bracketed serifs, and strong capital letters. Other than small book text, where the thin lines would suffer, this charming, single-weight design is good for almost any kind of work.

ABCDEFGHIJKLM
NOPQRSTUVWXYZ
abcdefghijklm
nopqrstuvwxyz
1234567890&!?;:"*

S

S

Serif Gothic

The result of the joint efforts of Herb Lubalin and Tony DeSpigna. It looks like a monoline sans at first glance, but the thorn-like serifs, not to mention the idiosyncratic circular letterforms, set this six-weight family aside as a distinctive display face.

ABCDEFGHIJKLM
NOPQRSTUVWXYZ
abcdefghijklm
nopqrstuvwxyz
1234567890&!?;:"*

Serifa

Adrian Frutiger created Serifa in 1967, using his Univers sans-serif design as a model. It has strong, Egyptian slab serifs, but more traditional humanist letterforms that keep it legible in longer runs of text. Best suited for display, advertising, and similar uses.

ABCDEFGHIJKLM
NOPQRSTUVWXYZ
abcdefghijklm
nopqrstuvwxyz
1234567890@&!?;:"*

Signa Serif

Part of the huge Signa family designed by Ole Søndergaard, a Swedish designer and typographer. This font has Didone serif characteristics with shapes and quirks normally associated with the first decades of the 20th century, although this stylish face was actually created in 2005.

ABCDEFGHIJKLM
NOPQRSTUVWXYZ
abcdefghijklm
nopqrstuvwxyz
1234567890@&!?;:"*

Signature

This is a display typeface design based on Arthur Baker's Baker Signet from the mid-1960s. The forms are best used for shorter portions of text, although the restrained stroke weight of the Light weight and the design's large x-height generally keep it very legible.

ABCDEFGHIJKLM
NOPQRSTUVWXYZ
abcdefghijklm
nopqrstuvwxyz
1234567890@&!?;:"*

Stone Serif

Part of Sumner Stone's monumental typographic family, Stone Serif is a highly attractive Transitional face that is designed to work smoothly with the other Stone companion fonts, Stone Sans and Stone Informal. Use in all forms of typesetting, especially when multiple type styles are needed in one layout.

ABCDEFGHIJKLM
NOPQRSTUVWXYZ
abcdefghijklm
nopqrstuvwxyz
1234567890@&!?;:"*

Syndor

A typeface design that has many qualities of a sans serif, although there are subtle yet unarguably strong flat-trimmed serifs throughout the letterforms. Syndor has a clear humanist feel, and the one-sided serifs give it a calligraphic flavor.

ABCDEFGHIJKLM
NOPQRSTUVWXYZ
abcdefghijklm
nopqrstuvwxyz
1234567890@&!?;:"*

Tarquinius

Created by Norbert Reiners during 1995–1997, Tarquinius could almost be described as an "upright italic." Despite having nominally traditional upright forms, the lines and shapes have a cursive, almost casual feel. A display font with a difference, ideal when clarity must be combined with informality.

ABCDEFGHIJKLM
NOPQRSTUVWXYZ
abcdefghijklm
nopqrstuvwxyz
1234567890@&!?;:"*

The Antiqua

A design that manages to balance a traditional appearance in the lighter weights with an almost slab-serif construction at the black end of the family. There is a serious air throughout, and the seven weights with associated italics and small caps make this a formidable family.

ABCDEFGHIJKLM
NOPQRSTUVWXYZ
abcdefghijklm
nopqrstuvwxyz
1234567890@&!?;:"*

Tibere

A font with a light touch; it has restrained serifs and mild, unassuming characteristics. But Tibere also exudes a quiet confidence and general restraint—except in Tibere Regular Swash, which has gorgeous curves flowing from the capitals. Particularly useful for book and magazine work.

ABCDEFGHIJKLM
NOPQRSTUVWXYZ
abcdefghijklm
nopqrstuvwxyz
1234567890@&!?;:"*

Tiffany

This is a typeface with plenty of character. Designed by Ed Benguiat, it successfully blends aspects of Ronaldson and Caxton. Tiffany has an irrepressible flair that makes it stand out from the crowd, and the numerals are particularly impressive.

ABCDEFGHIJKLM
NOPQRSTUVWXYZ
abcdefghijklm
nopqrstuvwxyz
1234567890@&!?;:"*

Times New Roman

Created under the watchful eye of Stanley Morison in the early 1930s, the now ubiquitous Times New Roman was first used in The New York Times on October 3, 1932. It is based on Old Style fonts, and managed to be both more condensed and more legible than previous newspaper type designs.

ABCDEFGHIJKLM
NOPQRSTUVWXYZ
abcdefghijklm
nopqrstuvwxyz
1234567890@&!?;:"*

Trajan

An interpretation of first-century Roman carved inscriptions on the Trajan columns. Its designer, Carol Twombly, completed the character set with numerals and punctuation and a bold variant but no lowercase. The clarity and presence of this titling font does justice to the original inscriptions.

ABCDEFGHIJKLM
NOPQRSTUVWXYZ
ABCDEFGHIJKLM
NOPQRSTUVWXYZ
1234567890@&!?;:"*

T

T

Tresillian

Tresillian Roman is a distinctly cursive font with an unusually small x-height and distinct pen-stroke qualities to the otherwise traditional letterforms. It sets fairly well at small sizes, but works best when the letterforms are large enough to be distinct. Consider combining with Tresillian Script.

ABCDEFGHIJKLM
NOPQRSTUVWXYZ
abcdefghijklm
nopqrstuvwxyz
1234567890@&!?;:"*

Truesdell

Designed by Frederic Goudy in 1930, all the drawings and matrices for Truesdell were lost when his studio burned down in 1939. Over half a century later it was redrawn using printed examples from the Rochester Institute of Technology, rescuing this elegant and delicately proportioned typeface design from obscurity.

ABCDEFGHIJKLM
NOPQRSTUVWXYZ
abcdefghijklm
nopqrstuvwxyz
1234567890@&!?;:"*

Trump Mediäval

Designed by Georg Trump in the 1950s, this face has crisp, angular elements that give text a sharp clarity on the page. It was intended to remain legible even on low-quality stock, and as a result it works well even at exceptionally small sizes on paper and screen.

ABCDEFGHIJKLM
NOPQRSTUVWXYZ
abcdefghijklm
nopqrstuvwxyz
1234567890@&!?;:"*

Usherwood

This font was created by Leslie Usherwood in 1984 for use as a display font and for short portions of text. Following classical type traditions, the ascenders are a little taller than the capitals, but the large x-height, not to mention the slightly organic curves, give this an individual feel.

ABCDEFGHIJKLM
NOPQRSTUVWXYZ
abcdefghijklm
nopqrstuvwxyz
1234567890&!?;:"*

Veljovic

Influenced in part by the work of Hermann Zapf, Veljovic's designer, Jovica Veljovic, has produced a crisp, beautifully crafted family that has just enough calligraphic verve to give text an unexpected spark of life on the page. Generous counters and serifs keep type legible in both small and large setting.

ABCDEFGHIJKLM
NOPQRSTUVWXYZ
abcdefghijklm
nopqrstuvwxyz
1234567890@&!?;:"*

Versa

Designed by Günther Flake in 2006, Versa straddles the line between serif and sans-serif. Letters are essentially monoline in construction, with some stroke cuts that imply a distant calligraphic origin, while the tiny flared serifs are only apparent when used at reasonably large sizes.

ABCDEFGHIJKLM
NOPQRSTUVWXYZ
abcdefghijklm
nopqrstuvwxyz
1234567890@&!?;:"*

Walbaum

This is an example of some of the finest 19th-century German type design, being a Modern-style Didone with vertical stresses and a slight squareness to the forms, but retaining a delicate grace even in the heavier weights. Superb for fine magazine and display typography.

ABCDEFGHIJKLM
NOPQRSTUVWXYZ
abcdefghijklm
nopqrstuvwxyz
1234567890@&!?;:"*

Warnock Pro

Named after John Warnock, cofounder of Adobe Systems, this design by Robert Slimbach balances classicism and contemporary forms in an exceptionally flexible body, caption, and display family. The wide variety of weights and optical size variants allows for meticulous design and typesetting control.

ABCDEFGHIJKLM
NOPQRSTUVWXYZ
abcdefghijklm
nopqrstuvwxyz
1234567890@&!?;:"*

Weidemann

This was originally named Biblica, as it was created as part of a collaborative project between the Catholic and Protestant churches to publish a bible. It was designed to be economical with space, retaining legibility and readability throughout large swathes of text.

ABCDEFGHIJKLM
NOPQRSTUVWXYZ
abcdefghijklm
nopqrstuvwxyz
1234567890@&!?;:"*

Winchester

A design by William Addison Dwiggins and Jim Spiece, Winchester is based on original Venetian type designs and has a curiously soft quality produced by the rounding off of all corners and stroke terminals. This makes an excellent book face when an old-fashioned feel is desired.

ABCDEFGHIJKLM
NOPQRSTUVWXYZ
abcdefghijklm
nopqrstuvwxyz
1234567890@&!?;:"*

Worcester

This typeface is based on normal Transitional forms, but with some characteristics, such as those in the g and number 7, that are rooted in the 20th century. Use mainly for regular text work, but consider this for some advertising uses as well.

ABCDEFGHIJKLM
NOPQRSTUVWXYZ
abcdefghijklm
nopqrstuvwxyz
1234567890@&!?;:"*

Zapf Renaissance

Drawn by Hermann Zapf from 1984–1986, it was created for phototypesetting requirements. It is actually a development on Zapf's own Palatino family from 40 years earlier, and provides optically scaled variants for use at different sizes, plus a broad range of typographic extras.

ABCDEFGHIJKLM
NOPQRSTUVWXYZ
abcdefghijklm
nopqrstuvwxyz
1234567890@&!?;:"*

Z

Akzidenz-Grotesk

This is a precursor to Helvetica; its wide range of widths and weights made it popular with German newspapers and magazines. Designed in the pre-digital, pre-film era, it is a classic of the postwar sans-serif style. It is highly functional, with clean lines, but lacks a huge amount of character.

A

ABCDEFGHIJKLM
NOPQRSTUVWXYZ
abcdefghijklm
nopqrstuvwxyz
1234567890@&!?;:"*

Alternate Gothic

A text and display font drawn by Morris Fuller Benton in 1903. A classic American condensed sans serif, it owes much more to Grotesque forms than to the geometric designs that were beginning to emerge in Europe at the time. It remained popular well into the latter half of the 20th century.

ABCDEFGHIJKLM
NOPQRSTUVWXYZ
abcdefghijklm
nopqrstuvwxyz
1234567890@&!?;:"*

Antique Olive

An idiosyncratic feature of this face is that the finials end vertically—in most fonts they are at right angles to the bowl. Its squarish, open design with a large x-height makes it readable at fairly small sizes. In addition to light, roman, and bold there are two condensed variants and and extended ultra bold version called Nord.

ABCDEFGHIJKLM
NOPQRSTUVWXYZ
abcdefghijklm
nopqrstuvwxyz
1234567890@&!?;:"*

Armada

Armada consists of 15 styles, most of which the condensed variants are most elegant. A square font but with curved tops and bottoms for each character, it looks handsome when set in capitals with generous or even extreme tracking.

ABCDEFGHIJKLM
NOPQRSTUVWXYZ
abcdefghijklm
nopqrstuvwxyz
1234567890@&!?;:"*

Authentic Sans

A square design with curved tops and bottoms, Linotype Authentic Sans is reminiscent of Armada but with the addition of chamfered tops to the vertical stems. The k features an unusual diagonal stem that starts from the baseline, making it look like a v with a supporting prop.

ABCDEFGHIJKLM
NOPQRSTUVWXYZ
abcdefghijklm
nopqrstuvwxyz
1234567890@&!?;:"*'

Auto 3

It offers a massive range and there are Auto 1 and 2 to consider, too. The roman versions are fairly uneventful—except for the capital C, which features a stubby, vertical ear—but the italic is as wacky as they come, with a hand-drawn look and every glyph a surprise.

ABCDEFGHIJKLM
NOPQRSTUVWXYZ
abcdefghijklm
nopqrstuvwxyz
1234567890@&!?;:"*

Avant Garde

This was derived from Herb Lubalin's logo for the magazine of the same name. It was originally capitals only with a backslanting A and M and overlapping ligatures for several letter combinations. The upper-and lowercase versions are distinguished by very round letter-forms, and the capital G has an extra-wide horizontal bar.

ABCDEFGHIJKLM
NOPQRSTUVWXYZ
abcdefghijklm
nopqrstuvwxyz
1234567890@&!?;:"*

Bauhaus

With one of the most revered names in 20th-century design, Bauhaus has a lot to live up to. Evocative of the 1920s, it is based on a circular O. Many glyphs, such as the b and d, feature a break so the letterform is not completed, and both the capital and lowercase e are very unusual.

ABCDEFGHIJKLM
NOPQRSTUVWXYZ
abcdefghijklm
nopqrstuvwxyz
1234567890@&!?;:"*

Bell Centennial

Designed by Matthew Carter for use in telephone directories, each font in the family was designed for a particular purpose—Bell Centennial Name & Number, for example. Legibility and economy of space were the prime considerations, plus the ability to print on ultra-lightweight paper.

ABCDEFGHIJKLM
NOPQRSTUVWXYZ
abcdefghijklm
nopqrstuvwxyz
1234567890@&!?;:"*

Bell Gothic

Created for the Bell Telephone Company's directories by Chauncey Griffith in 1938, this sans-serif was exceptionally legible at small sizes in letterpress output on relatively crude stock. Although it has been superseded by Bell Centennial (designed for litho print conditions), it is still an excellent, space-efficient face.

ABCDEFGHIJKLM
NOPQRSTUVWXYZ
abcdefghijklm
nopqrstuvwxyz
1234567890&!?;:"*

Benguiat

One of the most prolific type designers of the second half of the 20th century, Ed Benguiat gave his name to this font and its companion serif version. It is a curious design, with a modern look but with shapes like the capital A and B reminiscent of Art Nouveau.

ABCDEFGHIJKLM
NOPQRSTUVWXYZ
abcdefghijklm
nopqrstuvwxyz
1234567890@&!?;:"*

Bliss

Designed by Jeremy Tankard, one of the most respected type designers working today, Bliss Pro is both beautiful and practical. Within each weight are alternative sets of aligning and non-aligning numerals, small capitals, and ligatures, and it sets well in both text and display sizes.

ABCDEFGHIJKLM
NOPQRSTUVWXYZ
abcdefghijklm
nopqrstuvwxyz
1234567890@&!?;:"*

B

Bodega Sans

A charismatic font, and, as the name suggests, slightly nostalgic. All nine variants are condensed and have a fairly low center of gravity, the crossbar of the capital E and H being well below the center of the glyph. There are only three weights but each has non-aligning numerals and small capitals.

ABCDEFGHIJKLM
NOPQRSTUVWXYZ
abcdefghijklm
nopqrstuvwxyz
1234567890@&!?;:"*

Calibri

A ClearType font designed by Lucas de Groot to give better type rendering on LCD screens, Calibri is now included with Windows Vista, and Microsoft Office. It contains both aligning and non-aligning numerals and has slightly rounded corners. There are just four basic variants.

ABCDEFGHIJKLM
NOPQRSTUVWXYZ
abcdefghijklm
nopqrstuvwxyz
1234567890@&!?;:"*

Casablanca

With many variants, including several useful Condensed weights, Casablanca has a retro styling and some interesting glyphs—for example, the hybrid single/double-storey lowercase g with an ear that penetrates the bowl, and the eccentric lowercase m.

ABCDEFGHIJKLM
NOPQRSTUVWXYZ
abcdefghijklm
nopqrstuvwxyz
1234567890@&!?;:"*

Case Study

Similar in style to Briem Akademi but with six weights, all of them with the same condensed style, plus an Alternate version for each that includes non-aligning numerals and some ligatures. Case Study is a modern square font better suited to display than text.

ABCDEFGHIJKLM
NOPQRSTUVWXYZ
abcdefghijklm
nopqrstuvwxyz
1234567890@&!?;:"*

Channel 4

Created by Fontsmith for Channel 4 TV as part of the channel identity, its simplified shapes were conceived to work well on screen but it is a surprisingly good font for print applications roo, particularly at display sizes.

ABCDEFGHIJKLM
NOPQRSTUVWXYZ
abcdefghijklm
nopqrstuvwxyz
1234567890@&!?;:"*

Chianti

With its chiseled look and tapered stems, Chianti is extremely versatile for a sans serif. It includes three weights, each with italics; the wonderful Chianti Italic Swash; so-called Extension sets with ligatures, additional fractions, and even some decoration glyphs; and Alternate sets with special character adaptations.

ABCDEFGHIJKLM
NOPQRSTUVWXYZ
abcdefghijklm
nopqrstuvwxyz
1234567890@@&!?;:"*

C

Cholla

With just three weights, Cholla Sans is limited but there is an additional Wide series. It is a contemporary square font from the Emigre stable—who, for some inexplicable reason, have replaced the lowercase e with a small capital E in the Wide Ultra Bold variant, which also includes alternative non-aligning numerals.

ABCDEFGHIJKLM
NOPQRSTUVWXYZ
abcdefghijklm
nopqrstuvwxyz
1234567890@&!?;:"*

Coupe

Bangkok-based designer Anuthin Wongsunkakon drew Coupe in 2006. The slightly squared-off forms of this four-weight family are very well crafted, and although it is a little too idiosyncratic for small text it is ideal for modernist display and advertising work.

ABCDEFGHIJKLM
NOPQRSTUVWXYZ
abcdefghijklm
nopqrstuvwxyz
1234567890@&!?;:"*

Dax

Comprises a staggering 50-plus variants that includes expert sets, special characters, additional fractions, and ligatures Dax offers not just quantity but quality, too. Every weight is perfectly balanced with the rest; it is modern in style, and slightly condensed in its Regular version.

ABCDEFGHIJKLM
NOPQRSTUVWXYZ
abcdefghijklm
nopqrstuvwxyz
1234567890@&!?;:"*

Dieselis

A square font, the defining feature of which are the top bars that overlap to the left of the stem. It is available in only three weights, but each has italic and small capitals variants, and there is a companion family, Deselis Economic, that is condensed but has no small capitals.

ABCDEFGHIJKLM
NOPQRSTUVWXYZ
abcdefghijklm
nopqrstuvwxyz
1234567890@&!?;:"*

DIN

Intended for signage, the original DIN family was unusual as the fonts varied in width but not weight. These were later redeveloped by FontFont into a more conventional 30-strong family of varying weights that all retain the clarity and legibility of the original. The condensed variants are of particular merit.

ABCDEFGHIJKLM
NOPQRSTUVWXYZ
abcdefghijklm
nopqrstuvwxyz
1234567890@&!?;:"*

Eureka Sans

With a good range of weights in regular and condensed widths, Eureka Sans shares the basic design with its monospaced cousin but has many additional features. Non-aligning numerals are standard but if you require an aligning set, they can be found in the small capitals versions.

ABCDEFGHIJKLM
NOPQRSTUVWXYZ
abcdefghijklm
nopqrstuvwxyz
1234567890@&!?;:"*

Eurostile

This started life as a capitals-only display font that looked very modern in the 1950s when it was designed. A lowercase version and additional weights and widths were added later. In its classic extended version it doesn't look out of place among the square fonts that are popular today.

ABCDEFGHIJKLM
NOPQRSTUVWXYZ
abcdefghijklm
nopqrstuvwxyz
1234567890@&!?;:"*

Exemplar

Finally completed by Göran Söderström in 2008, Exemplar took 14 years to produce. It is built using classical proportions, but is characterized by its minimal use of serifs and a delicate and unusual set of alternate characters. It includes many context-sensitive and discretionary letterforms.

ABCDEFGHIJKLM
NOPQRSTUVWXYZ
abcdefghijklm
nopqrstuvwxyz
1234567890@&!?;:"*

Fago

Fago is a contemporary OpenType font with a large x-height that is available in five weights, each with a vast array of glyphs including small capitals, non-aligning numerals, additional fractions, ligatures, arrows, roman numerals, bullets, and more.

ABCDEFGHIJKLM
NOPQRSTUVWXYZ
abcdefghijklm
nopqrstuvwxyz
1234567890@&!?;:"*

Fedra Sans

It was born as a corporate font for a German insurance company, and intended to be a "de-protestantized Univers," but the project was canceled before it was finished. Nevertheless, designer Peter Bilak completed the work and in 2001 released this highly legible, subtly humanist family.

ABCDEFGHIJKLM
NOPQRSTUVWXYZ
abcdefghijklm
nopqrstuvwxyz
1234567890@G!?;:"*

Folio

Created by Konrad Bauer and Walter Baum in 1957, Folio was originally intended to be a direct competitor to Helvetica. It didn't end up posing a threat, but as a result this sturdy Swiss sans-serif family has not suffered from overexposure and remains very usable.

ABCDEFGHIJKLM
NOPQRSTUVWXYZ
abcdefghijklm
nopqrstuvwxyz
1234567890@&!?;:"*

Franklin Gothic

Designed by Morris Fuller Benton before World War I, Franklin Gothic is a genuine classic. Starting life with Bold, Bold Condensed, and Bold Extra Condensed variants, it has been added to ever since, and now boasts of a massive range, including small capitals in some type foundries' versions.

ABCDEFGHIJKLM
NOPQRSTUVWXYZ
abcdefghijklm
nopqrstuvwxyz
1234567890@&!?;:"*

F

F

Fresco Informal Sans

As its name suggests, this font has a friendly, informal character thanks to loops at the bottom of many terminals and the curving stems of capital glyphs such as A and H. It has a good range of weights, including the noticeably extended Bold and Black variants. Non-aligning numerals are available in the FontShop version.

ABCDEFGHIJKLM
NOPQRSTUVWXYZ
abcdefghijklm
nopqrstuvwxyz
1234567890@&!?;:"*

Frutiger

A classic font named after its illustrious designer Adrian Frutiger. When set as a paragraph, there is no sans serif that looks more even or balanced. It works equally well at display sizes—no surprise, as it was originally designed for airport signage.

ABCDEFGHIJKLM
NOPQRSTUVWXYZ
abcdefghijklm
nopqrstuvwxyz
1234567890@&!?;:"*

Futura

Futura is one of the most enduring of all fonts. Its designer Paul Renner has been almost deified by this one achievement, as he didn't design many other fonts. The tough, industrial-style design bears the hallmarks of the Constructivist movement from which it emerged in 1927. The expert set is available from Neufville Digital.

ABCDEFGHIJKLM
NOPQRSTUVWXYZ
abcdefghijklm
nopqrstuvwxyz
1234567890@&!?;:"*

Gill Sans

This is another 20th-century masterpiece and has never been out of fashion, despite being 80 years old. The capital character widths vary: C, D, G, O, Q, and U are quite wide, while B, E, P, and S are narrower, but the result is perfect harmony. The lighter weights are excellent for text setting.

ABCDEFGHIJKLM
NOPQRSTUVWXYZ
abcdefghijklm
nopqrstuvwxyz
1234567890@&!?;:'"*

Golary Red

This is a family of condensed fonts with no italics; it has a range of five weights, each with additional small capitals and non-aligning numeral options. It is unsuited to paragraph text setting but works well for subheads and as a space-saving and dramatic headline font.

ABCDEFGHIJKLM
NOPQRSTUVWXYZ
abcdefghijklm
nopqrstuvwxyz
1234567890@&!?;:"*

Goudy Sans

Designed in the 1920s with just Light and Bold versions, subsequent additions to Goudy Sans include a useful Regular weight and a useless Hairline variant (in the LTC version). Although a sans-serif, the stems tend to fatten at each end, suggesting a vestigial serif.

ABCDEFGHIJKLM
NOPQRSTUVWXYZ
abcdefghijklm
nopqrstuvwxyz
1234567890&!?;:'"*

Helvetica

Designed in 1957 by Max Miedinger, Helvetica—along with Univers—is the most important font of the postwar period. The Neue version substantially revised the original blueprint and rationalized its naming and numbering conventions to include the 50-plus variants that now exist.

ABCDEFGHIJKLM
NOPQRSTUVWXYZ
abcdefghijklm
nopqrstuvwxyz
1234567890@&!?;:"*

Industria

One of the Neville Brody fonts that helped define magazine design in the 1980s, Industria contains many idiosyncratic characters, including the tailless lowercase t and the K with slight curves at the ends of the strokes. Although just a single font, there is an alternate set and an inline version.

ABCDEFGHIJKLM
NOPQRSTUVWXYZ
abcdefghijklm
nopqrstuvwxyz
1234567890@&!?;:"*

Interstate

Designed by Tobias Frere-Jones, Interstate was based on the signage alphabets of the United States Federal Highway System. There are 36 styles from Hairline to Ultra Black as well as a complementary set of condensed fonts. With its clipped terminal, the lowercase g is the font's signature character.

ABCDEFGHIJKLM
NOPQRSTUVWXYZ
abcdefghijklm
nopqrstuvwxyz
1234567890@&!?;:"*

Karbid

An otherwise unremarkable font, Karbid has a Display variant (above) with some striking characters. The capital A sets the tone with an overlapping crossbar and curved terminal, with several other glyphs following suit. The lowercase g and k add to the repertoire of distinctive characters.

ABCDEFGHIJKLM
NOPQRSTUVWXYZ
abcdefghijklm
nopqrstuvwxyz
1234567890@&!?;:"*

Kouros

When you finally get to design a menu for a Greek restaurant, then look no further than Kouros. Although it is severely limited in range it has non-aligning numerals as standard (though no small capitals). Avoid using it at text sizes; this font is only suited to headlines.

ABCDEFGHIJKLM
NOPQRSTUVWXYZ
abcdefghijklm
nopqrstuvwxyz
1234567890@&!?;:"*

Meta

Meta is one of the most important fonts to have been created this century. Designed by Erik Spiekermann, every character is perfect; it has a massive range, including a condensed series and even a complementary serif. Especially worthy of mention is the lowercase g—to see it is to love it.

ABCDEFGHIJKLM
NOPQRSTUVWXYZ
abcdefghijklm
nopqrstuvwxyz
1234567890@&!?;:"*

M

Microgramma

Microgramma is very close in style to Eurostile. Although there is a medium-width Microgramma, the classic version is the extended one that is available in Medium and Bold weights. When it is set in text it produces a very strong horizontal linear pattern. There is no italic variant.

ABCDEFGHIJKLM
NOPQRSTUVWXYZ
abcdefghijklm
nopqrstuvwxyz
1234567890@&!?;:"*

Myriad

With 40 fonts in the family, Myriad was designed by two of the leading figures in modern type design, Robert Slimbach and Carol Twombly. Its glyph set is a staggering 800-plus per font, making it a clear choice for multi-language setting, and it offers Condensed and Semi Condensed (below) as well as Semi Extended options.

ABCDEFGHIJKLM
NOPQRSTUVWXYZ
abcdefghijklm
nopqrstuvwxyz
1234567890@&!?;:"*

News Gothic

Designed before World War II by the illustrious Morris Fuller Benton, News Gothic is a font without frills or pretension, but one that looks very elegant when set as paragraphs. It is slightly condensed with a fairly large x-height (see comparison with Futura) that gives it a sense of openness, particularly in its lighter variants.

ABCDEFGHIJKLM
NOPQRSTUVWXYZ
abcdefghijklm
nopqrstuvwxyz
1234567890@&!?;:"*

Officina Sans

Another font from the Erik Spiekermann stable at Meta Design, Officina Sans was designed to complement Officina Serif. With numerous additions to the original design, the family now comprises 25 fonts. Its condensed form and elegant design make it a very versatile face that can be used in almost any situation.

ABCDEFGHIJKLM
NOPQRSTUVWXYZ
abcdefghijklm
nopqrstuvwxyz
1234567890@&!?;:"*

Optima

Created in 1958 by Hermann Zapf, Optima betrays the calligraphic origins of its designer in its subtly waisted stems. It is often described as a font that straddles the divide between serif and sans serif and is invariably used to convey elegance and effortless style.

ABCDEFGHIJKLM
NOPQRSTUVWXYZ
abcdefghijklm
nopqrstuvwxyz
1234567890@&!?;:"*

Oxalis

Oxalis is wonderfully exotic; it contains some highly eccentric glyphs—notably the lowercase g and the ampersand—and the tops of many stems appear as if they were made by the flick of a brush. The non-aligning numerals are squat as Oxalis has a small x-height.

ABCDEFGHIJKLM
NOPQRSTUVWXYZ
abcdefghijklm
nopqrstuvwxyz
1234567890@&!?;:"*

Plastik

This is a condensed, squarish font but with heavily rounded corners. It comes in just two weights, but both have Italic and Alternate versions. More interesting is the Fantasy variant, where the stems of some characters are half rounded and the counters extended in the corners.

ABCDEFGHIJKLM
NOPQRSTUVWXYZ
abcdefghijklm
nopqrstuvwxyz
1234567890@&!?;:"*

Profile

An unflashy but very businesslike family of 40 fonts. It contains a wide range of expert characters, mathematical symbols, and alternate sets of numerals, and even includes alternative ampersands. The compact, space-saving design is maintained even in the Black variant.

ABCDEFGHIJKLM
NOPQRSTUVWXYZ
abcdefghijklm
nopqrstuvwxyz
1234567890@)&!?;:"*

Quay Sans

This is a sophisticated design that abounds with subtle features like the slightly splayed ends to all the straight strokes and the faintly angular curves of the bowls. Designed by respected designer David Quay, it has four weights and a quite steeply angled italic.

ABCDEFGHIJKLM
NOPQRSTUVWXYZ
abcdefghijklm
nopqrstuvwxyz
1234567890@&!?;:"*

Sassoon Sans

Initially developed by handwriting expert Dr. Rosemary Sassoon to help children learn to read and write, the family comprises Infant, Primary, and Sans. The exaggerated exit strokes have been removed from the Sans version (designed for more mature readers), which has longer ascenders and descenders.

ABCDEFGHIJKLM
NOPQRSTUVWXYZ
abcdefghijklm
nopqrstuvwxyz
1234567890@&!?;:"*

Scala Sans

Designed by Martin Majoor to complement Scala, Scala Sans is an elegant font with a range of 20 styles. It has long descenders including the lowercase j and y, which also feature a flattened curve in their tails. The OpenType versions include a massive 669 glyphs offering every conceivable extra character.

ABCDEFGHIJKLM
NOPQRSTUVWXYZ
abcdefghijklm
nopqrstuvwxyz
1234567890@&!?;:"*

Seria

Another font by Martin Majoor, Seria is characterized by extremely tall ascenders, and an italic that has the barest slant and is much more condensed than its roman equivalent. Non-aligning numerals are standard and there is a small capitals expert set for the both of the two weights available.

ABCDEFGHIJKLM
NOPQRSTUVWXYZ
abcdefghijklm
nopqrstuvwxyz
1234567890@&!?;:"*

Syntax

Designed by Hans Eduard Meier in 1968, Syntax was created for metal typesetting but has been updated, first for film and now for digital technology, largely by Meier himself. Its original design fundamentals have stood the test of time. It has five weights including an Ultra Black.

ABCDEFGHIJKLM
NOPQRSTUVWXYZ
abcdefghijklm
nopqrstuvwxyz
1234567890@&!?;:" *

TheSans

TheSans shares capitals and numeral glyphs with TheMix; in fact, the only characters that change are those that have serifs in TheMix—does this justify having two massive families? Whatever your views, TheSans is another masterpiece of type design, both elegant and functional.

ABCDEFGHIJKLM
NOPQRSTUVWXYZ
abcdefghijklm
nopqrstuvwxyz
1234567890@&!?;:"*

Transport

Designed in 1963 by Margaret Calvert and Jock Kinneir for British road signage, Transport was designed with optimum legibility as its goal. With a large x-height, it has just two weights, Medium and Bold, and no italic. It was clearly influenced by Helvetica.

ABCDEFGHIJKLM
NOPQRSTUVWXYZ
abcdefghijklm
nopqrstuvwxyz
1234567890&!?;:"*

Unit

From the stable of Erik Spiekermann comes another monster comprising 50-plus styles. Unit is a slightly condensed, straight-sided font with a range from Thin to Ultra Black and a parallel rounded version. It has very shallow non-aligning numerals as standard plus all the extras you would expect.

ABCDEFGHIJKLM
NOPQRSTUVWXYZ
abcdefghijklm
nopqrstuvwxyz
1234567890@&!?;:"*

Univers

If there was ever a granddaddy of sans serif fonts, Univers would be it. Originally designed as a 21-font family and released in 1957, it has been added to ever since, but without the radical overhaul that Helvetica received with Helvetica Neue. Its designer, Adrian Frutiger, was the first to name his fonts using a numerical system.

ABCDEFGHIJKLM
NOPQRSTUVWXYZ
abcdefghijklm
nopqrstuvwxyz
1234567890@&!?;:"*

Vag Rounded

Designed by Gerry Barney in 1979 as the corporate typeface for Volkswagen, Vag, as its name suggests, features rounded ends to all strokes. Its informal style was a rather surprising choice for a German motor manufacturer. It has four weights but no italic.

ABCDEFGHIJKLM
NOPQRSTUVWXYZ
abcdefghijklm
nopqrstuvwxyz
1234567890@&!?;:"*

V

A

Aachen

This unconventional Egyptian is available in two weights, Medium and Bold. The low contrast of stem thickness and stubby serifs make it capable of powerful imagery. Originally designed as part of Letraset's dry transfer library, it was created by John Brignall and Alan Meeks during the years 1969–1977 and digitized later by ITC.

ABCDEFGHIJKLM
NOPQRSTUVWXYZ
abcdefghijklm
nopqrstuvwxyz
1234567890&!?;:"*

American Typewriter

A popular, refined interpretation of the traditional typewriter letterform. Joe Kaden and Tom Stan's 1974 design is available in Light, Medium, and Bold, plus Condensed versions. The forms have been proportionally spaced but retain the immediacy that typewritten text evokes.

ABCDEFGHIJKLM
NOPQRSTUVWXYZ
abcdefghijklm
nopqrstuvwxyz
1234567890&!?;:"*

Bernhard Bold Condensed

Created by the German poster designer Lucian Bernhard in 1937, it was originally named Bernhard Antique Bold Condensed. It has a large x-height and small descenders. While the broad vertical stems predominate, it contains subtle detailed forms, making it an attractive choice for tight headings.

ABCDEFGHIJKLM
NOPQRSTUVWXYZ
abcdefghijklm
nopqrstuvwxyz
1234567890&!?;:"*

Bodoni Poster

The high-contrast thick-and-thin forms of Giambattista Bodoni's 18th-century types have survived many typographic developments since their first revivals in the 20th century. Now there are digital reworkings of Morris Fuller Benton's 1911 cutting, Heinrich Jost's 1926 cutting, and Chauncey H. Griffith's 1929 Bodoni Compressed, among others.

ABCDEFGHIJKLM
NOPQRSTUVWXYZ
abcdefghijklm
nopqrstuvwxyz
1234567890@&!?;:"'*

BottleKaps

This is a highly stylized display font with distinct echoes of 1920s and 1930s graphics. It is, however, a relatively modern creation, drawn in 1992 by Alex Kaczun. BottleKaps is suitable for high-impact display and advertising work, but despite extremely heavy shapes it has a surprisingly buoyant feel.

ABCDEFGHIJKLM
NOPQRSTUVWXYZ
abcdefghijklm
nopqrstuvwxyz
1234567890@&!?;:"*

Calcite

This Adobe font is a striking contemporary sans serif that hovers between roman and italics, giving it dynamic energy. Type designer Akira Kobayashi has used the contrasting forms of curves and rectangles to evoke the mineral forms that provide the font's title.

ABCDEFGHIJKLM
NOPQRSTUVWXYZ
abcdefghijklm
nopqrstuvwxyz
1234567890@&!?;:"*

C

Caslon Titling

This elegant engraved font with a tiny x-height is based on Caslon's classic font but is not from his foundry. Issued by Barnhart Bros. & Spindler in 1915, it originates from the G. Peignot foundry in France. Its classical elegance is useful where more subtle and refined display is required.

ABCDEFGHIJKLM
NOPQRSTUVWXYZ
abcdefghijklm
nopqrstuvwxyz
1234567890&!?;:""*

Compacta

This bold, condensed sans serif functions well in large sizes with tight letterspacing, creating powerful typographic impact. It was designed by Fred Lambert in 1963 for the Letraset dry transfer library, when condensed sans serifs were in great demand and printing was still predominantly black and white.

ABCDEFGHIJKLM
NOPQRSTUVWXYZ
abcdefghijklm
nopqrstuvwxyz
1234567890&!?;:"*

Confidential

Just van Rossum's Confidential is a caps only font that was designed to look like worn out, partly inked rubber stamp characters. It is highly condensed and suited to headlines and display work.

ABCDEFGHIJKLM
NOPQRSTUVWXYZ
1234567890
@&!?;:"*

C

Cooper Black

This is the extra bold version of Cooper Old Style, although it stands independently as a very popular font. It was created by Oswald Bruce Cooper, partner in a Chicago design firm, in 1919. Its bold friendliness provoked a trend in display fonts and has enjoyed several revivals.

ABCDEFGHIJKLM
NOPQRSTUVWXYZ
abcdefghijklm
nopqrstuvwxyz
1234567890@&!?;:" *

Cottonwood

An Adobe font, inspired by the decorative woodletter fonts of the 19th century. The basic letterform has been disguised by the decorative enhancement of the horizontal stress, rather than the conventional vertical stress. A font suited to a Wild West or Victoriana project.

ABCDEFGHIJKLM
NOPQRSTUVWXYZ
1234567890&!?;:"*

Dynamoe

A novelty capitals font reproducing a mechanical labelling system. Reversed out of black, the letters appear glossy and raised from the surface, but are not sharply defined. Designed by Just van Rossum in 1992, the font expresses spontaneity or transience.

ABCDEFGHIJKLM
NOPQRSTUVWXYZ
1234567890&

D

E

Edition

This freely downloadable font from dafont.com is an ultra condensed alphabet of extremely elegant capitals. The high contrast of stem and hairline serif makes it a suitable font for fashion or cosmetic advertising. The designer is unnamed.

ABCDEFGHIJKLM
NOPQRSTUVWXYZ
1234567890@&!?;:"*

Ed Roman

This font takes a traditional Didone-style design, albeit with exaggerated serifs, and puts a spring in it's step. The characters have a cavalier attitude to the baseline and many strokes sit at different heights.

ABCDEFGHIJKLM
NOPQRSTUVWXYZ
abcdefghijklm
nopqrstuvwxyz
1234567890@&!?;:"*

Ironwood

Ironwood, a 1990 font emulating a 19th-century woodletter display type, was created by Joy Redick for Adobe. This titling font features sharp pointed foot and head terminals reminiscent of gothic blackletter. The design suggests the Wild West or something spooky.

ABCDEFGHIJKLM
NOPQRSTUVWXYZ
1234567890&!?;:"*

Juniper

Designed in 1990 by Joy Redick for Adobe, Juniper expresses all the bold, extrovert qualities of a 19th-century woodletter type. The majority of the letterforms are variations on the basic concave stem. A powerful set of letters with a tinge of Art Nouveau.

ABCDEFGHIJKLM
NOPQRSTUVWXYZ
1234567890
@&!?;:"*

LCD

A digital font of capitals that emulates the Liquid Crystal Display used on many digital watches and displays. Martin Wait's design for Letraset, released in 1991, is an excellent choice when a science-fiction or high-tech mood is to be conveyed.

ABCDEFGHIJKLM
NOPQRSTUVWXYZ
1234567890&!?;:"◆

Lunatix

A two-weight font from Californian digital foundry Emigre, designed by Zuzana Licko and Rudy VanderLans in 1988–9. The partial serifs integrate a number of unique geometric forms, which mark it as a typeface rather than lettering. It is a true product of a new technology.

ABCDEFGHIJKLM
NOPQRSTUVWXYZ
abcdefghijklm
nopqrstuvwxyz
1234567890a&!?;:"*

Machine

Machine is a two-weight font conceived in the early 1970s, that is totally devoid of curves. Designed by Americans Ronne Bonder and Tom Carnase, this letterform expresses an industrial mood. The compact, simple capitals function with great impact on posters, signage, and packaging.

ABCDEFGHIJKLM
NOPQRSTUVWXYZ
1234567890
&!?;:"*

Mason

This is a digital font that appeared in 1992, the work of accomplished British type designer Jonathan Barnbrook. Initially named Manson, it was renamed after a storm of typographical controversy. Recently there have been alternative characters added. Mason is a font of highly visual formality.

ABCDEFGHIJKLM
NOPQRSTUVWXYZ
1234567890&!?;:"✦

Matisse

In 1995, graphic designer Gregory Grey developed this informal font while preparing a supplement for a Paris newspaper. The irregular and alternative characters are reminiscent of Henri Matisse's late cut-paper works, and indicate a lively spontaneity.

ABCDEFGHIJKLM
NOPQRSTUVWXYZ
1234567890@®&!?;:"*

Mesquite

This is a single-style, titling font by Joy Redick. This 1990 font draws inspiration from woodletters of the previous century and the title implies connections with the landscape of the Mexico/US border area. A natural choice for conveying circus life or the Wild West.

ABCDEFGHIJKLM
NOPQRSTUVWXYZ
1234567890&!?;:"*

Mojo

Jim Parkinson created this titling font in 1995, prompted by his admiration for the flamboyant lettering of the golden days of the 1960s psychedelic posters from San Francisco. Use it where '60s style is a major consideration, not legibility.

ABCDEFGHIJKLM
NOPQRSTUVWXYZ
1234567890&!?;:"*

Mona Lisa

Mona Lisa, with its elegant, high-contrast thick-and-thin strokes and remarkably small x-height, was created in 1991 by Pat Hickson. It is an update of Albert Auspurg's 1930s Art Deco type for the Ludwig and Mayer foundry. A font with a strong personality, it should be used with care.

ABCDEFGHIJKLM
NOPQRSTUVWXYZ
abcdefghijklm
nopqrstuvwxyz
1234567890@&!?;:"*

Onyx

Onyx was designed in 1937 by Gerry Powell, director of typographic design at ATF. In 1955, Monotype produced it as a hot metal font. As a condensed modern, it evokes the classic elegance of Bodoni, and has proved to be a very popular advertising type.

ABCDEFGHIJKLM
NOPQRSTUVWXYZ
abcdefghijklm
nopqrstuvwxyz
1234567890&!?;:"*

Parisian

Designed in 1928 by Morris Fuller Benton, Parisian bears some similarity to Broadway, but is lighter on the page and has a very small x-height. Like Broadway, it is influenced by European geometric sans-serifs. It has an elegant style, filled with nostalgia.

ABCDEFGHIJKLM
NOPQRSTUVWXYZ
abcdefghijklm
nopqrstuvwxyz
1234567890&!?;:"*

Playbill

For many years, Playbill was the standard font for expressing the characteristics of 19th-century advertising. Designed in 1938 by Robert Harling, the emphasis is placed on the horizontal serif area at the head and foot of each letter.

ABCDEFGHIJKLM
NOPQRSTUVWXYZ
abcdefghijklm
nopqrstuvwxyz
1234567890&!?;:"*

Plaza

A stylized geometric sans-serif expressing an Art Deco influence. Special features are a uniform line thickness, full circular O and Q, and very condensed T, U, N, etc. Designed by Alan Meeks in 1975, Plaza should be used wherever the elegant style of the 1920s and '30s is required.

ABCDEFGHIJKLM
NOPQRSTUVWXYZ
1234567890
&!?;:"*

Princetown

An alphabet of heavy outlined capitals inspired by U.S. college sportswear. It was designed in 1981 for the Letraset dry transfer library by Dick Jones. These letterforms, created without curves, provide considerable impact for sports-related imagery as well as sportwear.

ABCDEFGHIJKLM
NOPQRSTUVWXYZ
1234567890&!?;:"❋

Rennie Mackintosh

An Art Nouveau letterform imitating the lettering of Scottish architect Rennie Mackintosh, it was drawn by in 1993 by Phillip Grimshaw and released in 1996. The double and triple crossbar are highly distinctive details that make this font difficult to associate with anything other than the Art Nouveau period.

ABCDEFGHIJKLM
NOPQRSTUVWXYZ
123456789O@&!?;:"*

T

Thunderbird

This 19th-century Tuscan wood-letter digital revival comes in two contrasting variants. Thunderbird Regular has expanded letterforms with bifurcated serifs, while Thunderbird Extra Condensed is at the other proportional extreme. Thunderbird's obvious ornamental Victorian style will dominate the appearance of any publicity.

ABCDEFGHIJKLM
NOPQRSTUVWXYZ
1234567890
&!?;:"'*

Tombstone

A geometric digital font with a resemblance to a 19th-century woodletter type. It is characterized by heavy horizontal strokes and serifs, combined with a diamond shape marking midway between the capital height and the baseline. Designed by Dan Zadorozny of Iconian Fontsit.

ABCDEFGHIJKLM
NOPQRSTUVWXYZ
1234567890!?;:

Trixie

Trixie takes the concept of replicating typewritten text to its logical extreme, delivering the ragged and furry characters typical of a mechanical typewriter in dire need of a good clean. Trixie Text mixes together the Light and muckier Plain weights, and Trixie Extra provides a lowercase with filled-in counters.

ABCDEFGHIJKLM
NOPQRSTUVWXYZ
abcdefghijklm
nopqrstuvwxyz
1234567890&!?;:"'*

Verve

Created by versatile designer Brian Sooy of Altered Ego Fonts, Verve is a condensed display face—available in seven weights, ranging from Extra Light to Extra Black—that seems to hark back to the 1980s heyday of Neville Brody and The Face magazine for inspiration. Potentially useful for product packaging and advertising purposes.

ABCDEFGHIJKLM
NOPQRSTUUWXYZ
abcdefghijklm
nopqrstuuwxyz
1234567890@&!?;:"*

Viva

Viva is a classically proportioned open face with nine variants. Only a part of the letters' open forms are emboldened as the weight increases, offering possibilities for interesting typographic effects. Designed by Carol Twombly in 1993 for Adobe.

ABCDEFGHIJKLM
NOPQRSTUVWXYZ
abcdefghijklm
nopqrstuvwxyz
1234567890@&!?;:"*

Waters Titling

This font consists of 12 variants, which include a wide range of elegantly proportioned roman fonts with excellent serif detail. Every area of display from book jacket through packaging to posters will be enhanced by this font. Designed in 1997 by Julian Waters.

ABCDEFGHIJKLM
NOPQRSTUVWXYZ
1234567890
@&!?;:"*

American Scribe

Created by Brian Willson in 2003, American Scribe is derived from the handwriting of Timothy Matlack, the scribe responsible for making copies of the American Declaration of Independence from Thomas Jefferson's original draft of 1771.

ABCDEFGHIJKLM
NOPQRSTUVWXYZ
abcdefghijklmnopqrstuvwxyz
1234567890@&!?;:"*

Aquiline

This is a flamboyant yet practical handwriting font based on the lettering of the 16th-century writing master Arrighi. It has large, graceful flourishes on some capitals, and combines a small x-height with very tall ascenders. Use when a historical handwriting effect is required.

A BC DEFG HIJKLM
NO PQRSTUVWXYZ
abcdefghijklmnopqrstuvwxyz
1234567890@&!?;:"*

Avalon

These flamboyant, sweeping letterforms have their origins in the 16th century. Avalon is a full-blown calligraphic font based on the work of Austrian Friedrich Neugebauer and realized as a digital font by American type designer Richard Lipton in 1995.

ABCDEFGHIJKLM
NOPQRSTUVWXYZ
abcdefghijklmnopqrstuvwxyz
1234567890@&!?;:"*

Ballantines Script

This excellent Copperplate script is available in seven weights, from Light to Heavy, offering a wide range of possible uses, from advertising to packaging. Designed by the Brendel Typestudio in 1974.

ABCDEFGHIJKLM
NOPQRSTUVWXYZ
abcdefghijklmnopqrstuvwxyz
1234567890&!?,:"

Ballerino

This is a calligraphic script with echoes of the 16th century. Its lowercase, although small, is very legible, making it suitable for short texts rather than just headlines. Designed by Austrian Victor Solt-Bittner in 1999.

ABCDEFGHIJKLM
NOPQRSTUVWXYZ
abcdefghij klmnopqrstuvwxyz
1234567890@&!?;:"

Bernhard Schoenschrift

This script, designed by Lucian Bernhard in 1925, is identical to Stephen Blake's Madonna Ronde. It is a French-influenced script with an unlinked lowercase and a small x-height.

ABCDEFGHIJKLM
NOPQRSTUVWXYZ
abcdefghijklmnopqrstuvwxyz
1234567890&!?;:"

Cezanne

This font is an attempt to reproduce the artist's personal handwriting. There are six styles that include additional swash characters and ligatures. It was created by Michael Want and James Grieshaber, and first released in 1996. Cezanne has the authenticity of real handwriting, and consequently the irregularities and ink spread sometimes make it difficult to read.

ABCDEFGHIJKLM
NOPQRSTUVW XYZ
abcdefghijklmnopqrstuvwxyz
*1234567890@&!?;:"**

Civilité

Civilité refers to a typeface cut by Robert Granjon in 1556 and intended to be a French answer to the italics developed during the Italian Renaissance. There are several digital versions currently available; Monotype's Civilité MJ was designed by George Thomas.

ABCDEFGHIJKLM
NOPQRSTUVWXYZ
abcdefghijklmnopqrstuvwxyz
1234567890&!?;:"*

Décor

Décor is a script with the formality of a copperplate script but more personality. Elegant, with a generously sized lowercase x-height, it was designed by Gennady Baryshnikov in 1989. It is based on a script designed ten years earlier by Moscow book designer Pavel Kuzanyan.

ABCDEFGHIJKLM
NOPQRSTUVWXYZ
abcdefghijklmnopqrstuvwxyz
1234567890&!?;:,

Edwardian Script

This is an excellent copperplate script, available in four styles, that expresses flamboyance as well as the dignity of the average copperplate script. Designed in 1994 by Edward Benguiat, the talented and prolific New York lettering artist.

ABCDEFGHIJKLM
NOPQRSTUVWXYZ
abcdefghijklmnopqrstuvwxyz
1234567890@&!?;:"*

Giambattista

A unique cursive script released in 2004. It was long-cherished concept of type designer Gert Wiescher, to design a script (which Bodoni did not) that expressed the aesthetics that made Giambattista Bodoni famous. The curling swashes are a tribute to the 18th-century typographic master.

ABCDEFGHIJKLM
NOPQRSTUVWXYZ
abcdefghijklmnopqrstuvwxyz
1234567890@&!?;:"*

Johann Sparkling

This is a digital font that reproduces the handwriting of an 18th-century gentleman. A convincing natural handwriting style but rather difficult to read, as the miniscules are very small. Designed by Austrian designer Victor Solt-Bittner in 1998.

ABCDEFGHIJKLM
NOPQRSTUVWXYZ
abcdefghijklmnopqrstuvwxyz
1234567890@&!?;:"*

Julia Script

This flowing cursive script with a tendency to obesity along the baseline was inspired by the exuberant, psychedelic 1970s. Designed by David Harris in 1983 for the Letraset dry transfer library, it was digitized by Elsner and Flake, and will add humor to any text.

ABCDEFGHIJKLM
NOPQRSTUVWXYZ
abcdefghijklmnopqrstuvwxyz
1234567890&!?;: "

Katfish

A genuinely zany freeform script. The letterform sparkles with eye-catching vigor. The cursive lowercase dances across the page. The angular erratic capitals fling baubles in the air. A unique script designed by Michael Gills in 1994 for Letraset.

ABCD EFGHIJKLM
NOPQRSTUVWXYZ
abcdefghijklmnopqrstuv
wxyz 1234567890&!?;:

Lassigue D'Mato

A font capturing the scratchy forms of personal communication. Designed by American lettering artist Jim Marcus in 1996, the font has a diminutive lowercase which, unless used in fairly large sizes, makes reading difficult. A good font for a really personal statement.

ABCDEFGHIJKLM
NOPQRSTUVWXYZ
abcdefghijklmnopqrstuvwxyz
1234561890&!?;: "

Pablo

A brush script that pays homage to (arguably) the greatest artist of the 20th century, Pablo Picasso. When he created this font in 1995, Trevor Pettit managed to capture the unique qualities and rich variety of form in the artist's personal hand.

ABCDEFGHIJKLM
NOPQRSTUVWXYZ
abcdefghijklmnopqrstuvwxyz
1234567890&!?;:"*

Shelley Script

A group of three closely related scripts inspired by the calligraphy of 18th-century writing master George Shelley. Designed by British type designer Matthew Carter, each font is named after a musical term—Allegro, Andante, and Volante—and provide varying degrees flourish. Released in 1972.

ABCDEFGHIJKLM
NOPQRSTUVWXYZ
abcdefghijklmnopqrstuvwxyz
1234567890&!?;:"*

Zapfino

This is more a DIY calligraphy kit than a conventional font. Herman Zapf, the leading calligraphic type designer, created four fonts, accompanied by ligatures and ornaments. The four versions can be intermixed, so that each word of text can be individually constructed to give a unique calligraphic outcome.

ABCDEFGHIJKLM
NOPQRSTUVWXYZ
abcdefghijklmnopqrstuvwxyz
1234567890@(&!?;:"*

A

Araby Rafique

Tehmina Rafique's design pushes droplet shapes into angled and reflected distortions. The larger shapes are linked by fine, tapering strokes and the letters lean in random directions. Its legibility is low but it has style.

Bang

This font is inspired by the work of Joan Miró. It is made from extravagant curls, small decorative circles and quick strokes, all drawn with the same confident thin line. To appreciate the detail David Sagorski's design is best used large.

Bertram

Designed in 1991 by Martin Wait, a British typographer with well-known logos such as Radio Times magazine and Alpen cereal to his credit, and inspired by circus lettering, Bertram is a strong, casual design with a comic-book titling feel.

ABCDEFGHIJKLM
NOPQRSTUVWXYZ
1234567890
&!?;: "*

Chiller

An inkblot typeface created with far more care than is immediately apparent, Andrew Smith's chaotic design is a compendium of blots, spatters, and sprays that come together to produce a surprisingly legible result. It also includes a number of alternate characters to keep things looking random.

ABCDEFGHIJKLM
NOPQRSTUVWXYZ
abcdefghijklm
nopqrstuvwxyz
1234567890&!?;:"*

Curlz

Jaunty to the point of exploding off the page, this has curls upon curls throughout the character set, justifying the name beyond any shadow of a doubt. It is difficult to use for more than a few words at a time, but in the right context it can look stunning.

ABCDEFGHIJKLM
NOPQRSTUVWXYZ
abcdefghijklm
nopqrstuvwxyz
1234567890@&!?;:"*

Dinitials Positive

Helga Jörgenson's font is a lush set of illustrated initials decorated with prehistoric lizards and fantastic creatures. This mid-1990s design could have come straight from a Victorian children's book.

ABCDEFGHIJKLM
NOPQRSTUVWXYZ
1234567890

D

Downtown

The highly compact forms of Downtown have two baselines: the lowercase forms sit centered within the height of the capital letters. The small, strong serifs, the art deco flavor, and their emphatic slant combine strength with typographic delicacy.

ABCDEFGHIJKLM
NOPQRSTUVWXYZ
abcdefghijklm
nopqrstuvwxyz
1234567890@&!?;:"*

Goodies

Goodies was created by Anne Boskamp in 2002. It consists of two faces Goodies A and B which contain highly illustrative renderings of characters. The designs bear similarities to some of Joan Miró's surrealist paintings.

ABCDEFGHIJKLM
NOPQRSTUVWXYZ
ABCDEFGHIJKLM
NOPQRSTUVWXYZ
1234567890&!?;:"*

Jokerman

Jokerman has a youthful energy and an almost cubist approach to decoration that enhances its sense of excitement. Designer Andrew Smith included a number of character alternatives and decorative graphic devices, so be sure to explore everything.

ABCDEFGHIJKLM
NOPQRSTUVWXYZ
abcdefghijklm
nopqrstuvwxyz
1234567890&!?;: 9**

Kismet

The ornamental Kismet is older than it looks. This decorative, geometrically constructed face was created by John Cummings in 1879 and repeats the graphic theme of circles, spirals and inner dots throughout the design.

A B C D E F G H I J K L M
N O P Q R S T U V W X Y Z
a b c d e f g h i j k l m
n o p q r s t u v w x y z
1 2 3 4 5 6 7 8 9 0 @ & ! ? ; : " A *

Masterpiece

This is exactly what the name implies. This is a fine script face drawn with a scratchy pen on paper that snags and blots. Masterpiece Andante is drawn slowly with style and swashes, Allegro is dashed off more quickly, while Initials and Expert give all the extras you could want.

A B C D E F G A I K L M
N O P Q R S T U V W X Y Z
a b c d e f g h i j k l m n o p q r s t u v w x y z
1 2 3 4 5 6 7 8 9 0 @ & ! ? ; : " *

Mr Frisky and Uncle Stinky

A curious pair. At first glance they seem identical, both having a cartoony anarchy to their hand-drawn serif shapes. On closer examination you'll see differences between most characters, giving Uncle Stinky a slightly broader and fractionally lighter feel on the page.

A B C D E F G H I J K L M
N O P Q R S T U V W X Y Z
a b c d e f g h i j k l m
n o p q r s t u v w x y z
1 2 3 4 5 6 7 8 9 0 @ & ! ? ; : " *

REFERENCE

Glossary

10

accent Mark added to a character to indication change of pronunciation.

aliasing Ragged rendering caused by digitizing subtle forms onto a fixed grid.

alphanumeric A full set of letters and figures, including punctuation.

antialiasing Shading applied to the jagged edge of a digital character to simulate smoothness.

aligned left (flush left, ranged left) The arrangement of lines of type so that the extreme left edges line up one under the other, leaving right hand edges ragged.

aligned right (flush right, ranged right)
The arrangement of lines of type so that the extreme right edges line up one under the other, leaving left hand edges ragged.

aligning numerals Numerals of the same height sitting on the baseline, usually same height as capitals.

alphanumeric set (character set) A complete set of letter, numerals, and punctuation.

ampersand The symbol (&) that abbreviates "and." Derived from "and per se and."

arabic numerals The numeric symbols: 1 2 3 4 5 6 7 8 9 0.

arm The short stroke leading away from a vertical within a character, as in "E," "F," "L."

ascender The part of certain lowercase letters that rises above the x-height.

auto leading The automatic insertion of interline spacing by most DTP applications, usually set at 20% of the body height.

baseline An imaginary line on which the bases of capitals and most lowercase letters rest.

baseline grid A temporary grid of horizontal lines at fixed intervals, adjusted as required.

baseline shift A DTP function allowing for some selected characters to display above or below the true baseline.

bézier curve A mathematical formula used to calculate the shape of a curve between two points (a vector).

bitmap A "map" describing the location and binary state (on, off) of bits. It defines a complete collection of pixels that comprise an image, such as a letter.

blackletter A 15th-century script from northern Europe, also called Gothic and Old English.

block A letterpress image photochemically etched or engraved onto a zinc or copper plate and mounted on a wood or metal base.

body The shank of a piece of metal type.

body text Typesetting forming the main portion of a book or other printed matter.

bold face A heavier variant of the normal roman of a given typeface.

bowl The curved or circular forms of characters, such as "O," "Q," "P, " or "d."

bracketed serif A serif that has an intermediary curve between the horizontal serif and vertical stroke.

brush script A typeface imitating an alphabet formed by brushstrokes.

calligraphy The art of fine writing, derived from the Greek words for beautiful writing: Kallos (beauty) and graphien (to write).

capitals Large letters that originate from Roman Square Capitals. Also known as Majuscules.

cap height The height of a capital alphabet in a given typeface.

centered A typographic arrangement which appears symmetrical on the page.

chancery script A script used by scribes in the Papal Chancery during the 15th and 16th centuries.

character set A complete set of letters, numerals, punctuation, and symbols in a font that constitutes a set of digital matrices.

cicero The European typographic unit. One Cicero is 12 Didot points.

colophon A printer or publisher's trademark.

composing stick A metal adjustable holder, within which the compositor assembles letters into lines of type.

composition The process of typesetting, whether by hand or machine.

composition size Type sizes up to 14 pt, also known as text size.

compositor A craftsman responsible for the setting of type by hand and machine, and making up pages.

condensed A typeface variant that is narrower than the basic roman font.

copperplate script A typeface based on the forms of 18th-century formal scripts, also used by engravers.

counter The enclosed or semi-enclosed white space in letters such as "o," and "e," the term derives from the counterpunch used to form the space.

crossed strokes Crossed strokes within a letterform as in "W."

crossbar Horizontal stroke of a letterform as in "H."

cursive A script or typeface with joined characters.

dash Small horizontal punctuation mark. Can be long or short but is longer than a hyphen.

descender The part of lowercase letters and some capitals that hangs below the baseline.

diacritical marks

Accents, dots, and other linguistic signs used to record special pronunciation.

didones The British Standards Type classification term for 18th-century "modern" types.

didot point The European unit of type measurement, established by François-Ambroise Didot in 1775. One Didot point is 0.351 mm; 12 Didot points make 1 Cicero.

die An intaglio engraved stamp used for impressing a design.

dingbat / wingding A non alphanumeric symbol. (Mac: Zapf Dingbats, Windows: Wingdings).

diphthong The combined vowels pronounced as one syllable: Æ, Œ.

display size Type sizes above 14-points.

drop capital A large initial capital letter at the beginning of a paragraph that occupies space on several lines .

ear The stroke attached to the upper bowl of "g," also used describe the curved stroke of the "r."

edition The complete number of copies of a work printed and issued at one time.

egyptian A slab-serif typeface that first made an appearance in the early 19th century.

ellipsis Term for three small dots following a line of text to indicate a break or pause...

em A unit of Anglo-American type measurement. An em is a square of any given body size, e.g. 12 x 12-points, 8 x 8-points.

em rule A dash used as punctuation; the length of one em.

en A unit of Anglo-American type measurement, which is half an em.

en space A word space that is a half an em space.

etching An intaglio process; it is an image or design in which incisions are created by the corroding act of acid on a metal plate.

exception dictionary A list of word breaks that are exceptions to the standard instructions stored in the computer.

expanded A typeface variant proportionally wider than the basic roman.

expert set An additional font of characters, extra to the standard character set. It can include non- aligning figures (OSF), small capitals (SC), fractions, and other signs.

eye The small enclosed counter shape in the letter "e."

face The visual identity of a typeface.

family The related weights, italics, condensed, and expanded forms of a typeface.

fat-face A 19th-century display type of dramatically heavy weight or thickness.

figures Type numerals.

film disc Early phototypesetting matrix where film negative letterforms were ranged around the edge of a spinning disc.

fist An index mark represented as a pointing hand.

fixed word-spacing Word-spacing in a passage of typesetting that is the same unit throughout; when set flush left it creates ragged line endings.

flush left Typesetting in which the lines are aligned on the left.

folio Page number.

font A complete set of characters, capitals, lower case, figures, and punctuation. In metal typesetting, a font consisted of a quantity of each character in proportion to other letters to fill a typecase.

forme Typesetting and printing blocks assembled into pages and locked into a chase ready to fit into the printing press.

frame A high bench used by compositors, which has a sloped top to support typecases while type is being set.

frontispiece An illustration on a verso page opposite the title page of a book.

full point A period.

galley proof A proof of typesetting before it is made into pages.

garalde Classification of the group of typefaces with strong, calligraphic (pen like) influences.
See also Old Face.

geometric sans-serif Sans-serif typefaces of the early 20th century; they are constructed by use of strict geometric single-line thickness forms.

glyph A shape of a character, accent, or symbol, irrespective of its name.

glyphic Typeface forms with a chiselled rather than calligraphic influence on their form.

gothic 1. Northern European letterform of the 15th century; also known as blackletter.
2. A term in the United States for sans-serifs.

grotesque A Sans-serif typeface of the 19th century.

hanging indent Where first lines of a paragraph start at a point to the left of the main alignment. Sometimes referred to as reverse indent.

hanging punctuation Where, for aesthetic reasons, punctuation may be placed marginally outside the perceived column width.

hard hyphen A user-placed hyphen that remains with the broken word or word liaisons wherever it may fall along a line.

heavy A variant of a type family, usually darker than bold.

hinting Instructions contained in a font to determine how to correct an outline that does not exactly fit a pixel grid. For example, when type appears on screen at low resolution.

h&js Hyphenation and Justification. The part of the computer program that deals with word breaks and word spacing.

hot metal Typesetting produced by letterpress typesetting machines such as Monotype, Linotype, and Ludlow type.

humanist Early-roman typefaces produced in Italy during the Renaissance.

humanist sans-serif Sans-serif typefaces whose form is based on inscriptional roman and humanist proportions. It usually has some stroke contrast, a two-storey "a," and a closed-loop "g."

hyphenation The breaking of words, ideally at the end of a syllable, in order to fit a measure.

hyphenation zone A user-definable area at the end of a line of type to force hyphenation to occur earlier or later depending on the value given.

imprint The information concerning copyright, printing, and publishing history of a book. Usually found on the reverse side of the title page.

indent A common method of identifying a paragraph by leaving a blank space at the start of a line.

inferior character A small character placed below the baseline, as in Co2 or to cross reference a footnote.

italic A companion typeface to roman, with a cursive appearance.

jaggies The visible stepping of pixels seen at low resolution as can be seen on monitors, for example.

justification The process of adjusting words and spaces to fit a measure.

kerning The adjustment of pairs or groups of letters to improve letterfit.

latin The standard alphabet used by Western European languages.

leader A row of small dots used to guide a reader across an area of white space to further text. E.g. from the entry on a "Contents" page across to the corresponding page number.

leading Interlinear spacing of lines of type. Originally strips of lead of various thicknesses.

leg The righthand, downward letter stroke found on "K" and "R." See also Tail.

legibility Refers strictly to whether letterforms can be easily distinguished—which may or may not necessarily contribute to readability.

letterfit The relationship of one letter to another in any combination.

letterpress A method of printing from a raised surface such as metal type, woodcuts, and linocuts.

ligature Tied letters of commonly reoccuring pairs such as "fi," "fl," "pt," and "ch."

light A fine weight variant in a family of typefaces.

lineale Classification of group of typefaces without serifs (sans-serif). See also Sans-serif.

link A stroke connecting the bowl and enclosed loop of the "g."

loop The enclosed descender of the letter "g."

lower case The small letters of a typeface, also known as miniscules.

majuscules See Capitals.

manuscript A hand-written document. More recently this refers to a document written or typed by an author before it is translated into type.

margins The white space between the printed area of a page and the trimmed edge. They consist of the head margin, the foot margin, the fore-edge margin, and the spine margin.

matrix A metal die from which a single type is made.

matrix store The electron storage of a typeface.

measure The width of a column to which a line of type is set.

medium Generally the primary weight of type family. Also called regular or roman.

metrics Values and units held in a font for controlling the accurate spacing of type on screen and when printed.

miniscules See Lower case.

minus leading The elimination of interlinear spacing so that the descenders and ascenders of two lines overlap.

minus letter-spacing The elimination of word-spacing to the degree that letters touch or overlap.

modern A common term to define typefaces with hairline serifs and strong vertical stress; originally developed in the late 18th century.

monoline An alphabet of letters with a single-line thickness.

monospaced An alphabet of letters of a single-unit width throughout.

mold An adjustable device in which a matrix is fitted in order to cast a single type.

non-aligning figures Figures based on the x-height of a typeface, which have ascenders and descenders.

normal letterspacing The letterfit of a typeface that is the set width of the original design.

oblique stroke A line sort, inclined right. Also called a shilling stroke or slash.

oblique A typeface that is a sloped roman rather than a true italic.

old english See Gothic.

old-face A style letterform used from the late 15th century to the middle of the 18th.

old-style A 19th-century adaptation of Old-face characteristics.

old-style figures See Non-aligning figures.

opentype Cross-platform font format allowing TrueType and Type 1 fonts to be enclosed in one "wrapper" and offering the possibility of a large character set.

ornaments Typographic sorts and borders used for decoration.

orphan The first line of a paragraph at the foot of a page or column.

outline A typeface formed as an outline rather than solid strokes.

pantograph A mechanical device for enlarging or reducing images.

paper tape A strip of paper on which data is recorded by a code of punched holes.

photocomposition The production of typesetting by use of a keyboard for input, and the use of a photo unit to produce output.

phototypesetting The produce of photocomposition; usually a bromide print.

pica A standard Anglo-American typographic unit, which is 12-points. Six picas equal one inch.

pi characters Special characters not included in a normal character set; also know as sorts. For example: mathematical signs, reference marks, and other symbols.

platen press A letterpress printing press in which a flat plate or platen is pressed against the horizontal forme.

point The basic typographic unit of measurement. It is a term used by both the Anglo-American and the European Didot system.

point size The body size of a typeface.

postscript Adobe's patent page description language; it enables vecto-based outlines to be rasterized efficiently.

prelims and postlims The material prior to the main text and following the main text in the structure of a book.

printers marks Marks used on a proof by the compositor or editor to identify mistakes and corrections required.

printing plate In offset lithography, a thin metal sheet wrapped around a cylinder holding the image to be printed.

proof A test printing, in order to check for quality at various stages prior to the print run.

punch A hardened stick of steel, which is engraved with a type character.

punchcutter The craftsman whose highly-skilled function is to engrave a set of punches required for each size of typeface.

quad 1. Letterpress spacing material.
2. Denotes a sheet of paper for printing, which is four times the size of the broadsheet.

ragged Typesetting that is aligned on the left with fixed word-spacing creating a ragged right alignment.

rasterization The conversion of outlines into dots.

readability Where consideration to layout, spacing, and choice of typeface make for comfortable, sustained reading.

regular See Medium.

river Name given to connecting ragged white spaces running downwards through lines of continuous text.

roman Regular upright style of typeface or character, as opposed to italic style of design.

rules Metal strips that are type height and print as lines.

run-around A column of text composition is adjusted to fit around what is generally an irregular-shaped illustration.

sans-serif A letterform that does not have serifs. See Grotesque.

script 1. A handwritten letterform.
2. A typeface that attempts to imitate such a letterform.

serif The short finishing stroke projecting from the end of a letter's stem. These consist of several varieties of form, and gives the type face its particular character.

set solid Text or display typesetting that has no additional interlinear spacing.

shadowed An additional thickness of line added to a letterform to suggest three dimensions.

side bearing The amount of space either side of characters to ensure that with normal setting they are adequately spaced apart.

slab-serif An early 19th-century typeform, with serifs of similar thickness to the stems; also called Egyptian.

sloped roman A typeface variant to the roman, with a lean to the right, as a substitute for an italic.

small caps An alphabet of capital letters that align with the x-height of a font.

soft return Has the effect of taking text onto a new line without the application considering it to be a new paragraph. Usually obtained by holding the Shift key down while pressing Return key.

sort(s) An individual character from a font; it also can be a special character not included in a font.

spine The main surved stroke of the "S."

spur A short spike on the base of the stem of a capital "G."

stem All vertical or near vertical full-length strokes of a character.

stress The vertical or angled direction or angle of a character's form.

stroke A line that forms part of a letter.

superior character Small characters set to appear near the capital height of a typeface.

superscript A small character that may be positioned at any point above the x-height. E.g. 30°.

symbol A graphic character that is neither alphanumeric or punctuation.

swash An exaggerated flourish given to some letterforms.

swell The thickening of a curved character stroke.

swash An ornamental capital letter for use with italic alphabets, available in upper case and lower case.

tabulation The setting of text or figures in the form of columnar tables, according to fixed measures.

tail The margin at the foot of a page. Also the curved terminal strokes of letters such as "Q," "R," "K." Also known as leg.

terminal The end of a letter stroke.

titling A capital typeface that has no descenders. In metal types this meant that the height of the letters could be increased to use the descender space.

thick and thin The contrast of stem thickness of a typeface.

tracking Amount of inter-character space over a range of characters.

transitional A typeface design of the 18th century with horizontal and pronounced stroke stress.

typecutter See Punchcutter.

type height The standard dimension of type from the foot to the face: 0.91".

type scale A rule used by compositors, calibrated in points and ems.

typesetting The product of type composition whether by metal, photosetting, or computer.

umlaut Accent comprising two small dots, placed above a character to denote special pronounciation.

unicode An international standard digital code for describing a character set.

u/lc Upper and lowercase. The combination of alphabets used in a piece of typesetting.

unit system A system in which each character of a font is given a fixed number of units to its width. The machine is able to calculate how many characters will fit a line.

unjustified A typeset column that is aligned flush on the left and ragged on the right.

upper case Also known as capitals.

venetians 15th-century serif typeface. Considered the first true humanist roman typeface, attributed to Nicholas Jenson c.1470.

weight The overall line thickness of a typeface, which creates the color on the page.

widow The last line of a paragraph or lone word at the top of a page or column.

wood engraving A method of creating a letterpress image by cutting it into the end grain of a block of hard wood; this method is capable of finer results than a woodcut.

word space The white space between words, which in metal typesetting was created by combinations of non-printing body-sized pieces of type metal. "Em," "En," "Thick," "Mid," "Thin."

x-height The main area of lowercase type that does not include ascenders and descenders.

Index

10

Acknowledgments

The publisher would like to thank the following individuals and organizations for their kind permission to reproduce the fonts in this book:

2Rebels: *Deselis, Plastik*; 3IP: *American Scribe*; Berthold: *City*; Bitstream: *Chianti, Cooper, Mirarae*; Chank: *Mr Frisky and Uncle Stinky*; DaFont.com: *Edition*; Elsner + Flake: *Ballantines Script, Bernhard Schoenschrift, Elysa, Excalibur, Julia Script, Kiev, Panther, Zapf Renaissance*; Font.Bureau: *Armada, Avalon, Bodega, Phaistos, Prensa*; FontFont: *Angie, Angkoon, Cellini, Confidential, Danubia, Dynamo, Eureka, Eureka Sans, Fago, Karbid, Masterpiece, Meta, Page Serif, Profile, Reminga, Scala, Scala Sans, Seria, Signa, Tarquinius, Tibere, Trizie, Unit*; Fontshop International: *Atma*; Fontsmith: *Channel 4*, Grouptype: *Aquiline*; Iconian Fonts: *Tombstone*; ITC: *Romana*; Jeremy Tankard Typography: *Bliss, Enigma*; Linotype: *Thunderbird, Worcester*; LucasFonts: *TheAntiqua, TheSans*; Microsoft Typography/Ascender Corporation: *Calibri*; Monotype: *Grantofte (Sans), Moteverde (Sans), Signature (Sans), Tresilian (Sans)*; P22: *Cezanne*; Paratype: *Decor, Haverj (Sans), Literaturnaya (Sans)*; Présence Typography: *Cicero, Kouros, Laricio*; Primetype: *Golary Red*; Psy/Ops: *Exemplar*, T.26: *Coupe*; Type Innovations: *BottleKaps*; Typotheque: *Fedra (Sans)*; Underware: *Auto 3*; URW: *Craw Modern*; Wiescher Design: *Giambattista*

2Rebels; 3IP; Berthold; Bitstream; Chank; DaFont.com; Elsner + Flake; Font Bureau; FontFont; Fontshop International; Fontsmith; Grouptype; Iconian Fonts; ITC; Jeremy Tankard Typography; Linotype; LucasFonts; Microsoft Typography/Ascender Corporation; Monotype; Paratype; P22; Présence Typography; Primetype; Psy/Ops; T.26; Type Innovations; Underware; URW; Wiescher Design

Monotype Imaging Ltd.
Unit 2, Perrywood Business Park,
Salfords, Redhill, Surrey RH1 5DZ, U.K.
Tel: +44 (0)1737 765959/ Fax: +44 (0)1737 769243
www.monotypefonts.com

Monotype Imaging Inc. (Corporate)
500 Unicorn Park Drive, Woburn, MA 01801
Tel: (781) 970-6000 / Fax:(781) 970-6001
Toll Free: (800) 424-8973, prompt 2
www.monotypeimaging.com

Monotype GmbH
Werner-Reimers-Straße 2-4,
D-61352 Bad Homburg, Germany
Tel: +49 (0) 6172 484-418 / Fax: +49 (0) 6172 484-429
www.linotype.com

p12 (L) British Library, London (R) Bibliotheque Nationale, Paris; p14 Biblioteca Nacional, Madrid; p15 (T) British Library, (B) Bodleian Library, Oxford; p19 Biblioteca Nacional/Joseph Martin; p35 Musee National des Techniques, Paris; p53 Theatre Museum, London; p108 (T) Cambridge University Library; other images from private collections.